INTRODUCTION
TO
SANKARA'S ADVAITISM

Introduction
To
Sankara's Advaitism

Amb. Dr. Prakash Joshi

**MOTILAL BANARSIDASS
INTERNATIONAL
DELHI**

Revised Edition : Delhi, 2023
First Edition : Delhi, 2006

ISBN : 978-81-19196-86-9

<u>*Also available at*</u>

MOTILAL BANARSIDASS INTERNATIONAL
H. O.: 41 U.A. Bungalow Road, (Back Lane)Jawahar Nagar, Delhi - 110007
4261 (Basement) Lane # 3, Ansari Road, Darya Ganj, New Delhi - 110002
12/1A, 2nd Floor, Bankim Chatterjee Street, Kolkata - 700073
Shop #. 6, 241, Luz Ginza Complex, Luz Corner, Mylapore, Chennai - 600004
Stockist : Motilal Books, Ashok Rajpath, Near Kali Mandir, Patna - 800004

Printed in India
MOTILAL BANARSIDASS INTERNATIONAL

Dedication

To Nalini
Who taught me
the meaning of life

Quotes

To him who knows the Truth comes the realisation:- 'I am Brahman: I have no suffering and no joy; I neither long for anything, nor do I renounce anything; I am blue, I am yellow, I am white; I am in grass, leaves, trees and flowers; I am the hills, the streams, dales and peaks; I am the essence of all. When all imagination and feelings are gone, then I am the transcendental reality. The immutable, the nameless and the formless, am I: I am the witness self; I am the basis of all experience; I am the light that makes experience possible'.

—Yoga Vasistha

Two birds that are ever associated and have similar names, cling to the same tree. Of these, one eats fruits of varied tastes, and the other looks on without eating....

"One the same tree, the individual soul remains entangled (i.e. stuck), as it were; and so it moans, being worried by its impotence. When it see thus the other, the adored Lord, and his glory, then it becomes liberated from sorrow."

—Monduka Upanisad

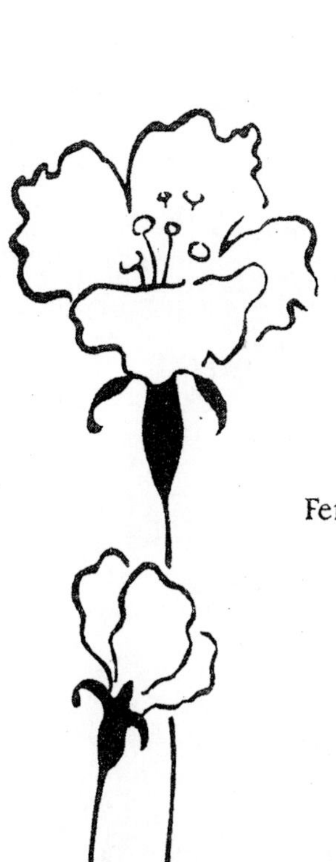

CONTENTS

FOREWORD

It gives me great pleasure to place this small book on Advaitism before the readers. Adi Sankara's philosophy on Advaitism is justly famous for its breadth of vision, universality of its scope and impeccability of its logic. This is the reason why Adi Sankara is revered as one of the topmost philosophers of Hinduism.

2. This book is divided into thirteen chapters and attempts to give a succinct overview of different facets of Advaitism. It contains a brief profile of Sankara's life. An entire chapter (No.3) has been devoted to the portrayal of evolution of metaphysical thought in India from earliest of times until Sankara emerged on the scene. The reader thus will be able to appreciate how Advaitism blends harmoniously into the ideas and concepts which were in vogue earlier. The main features of Advaitism have been explained on the basis of Sankara's seminal work 'Vivekchoodamani'.

3. Sankara is famous for his commentaries on the Gita, Upanisads and Brahmasutra. In view of the importance of these works, a separate chapter has been devoted to each of these commentaries. Despite the constraints of space, several quotations from Sankara's original works have been adduced so that the reader gets a flavour of Sankara's mode of argumentation as well as his unique literary style.

4. An attempt has been made to counter the two widely prevalent misconceptions about Advaitism in this publication. It is held by many that Sankara called for severing of links with the temporal world and for adoption of a monastic existence by one and all. It is said that he

import. It has been shown that this is far from correct. Sankara advocated Gyanyoga which is based on monasticism only for those saintly people who could cognize the transcendence of soul and differentiate it from the perishable body. He commended Karmayoga for the vast majority of the people who could not reach such a spiritual height.

5.   Secondly, it is also put forth that Sankara regarded the world as an illusion and this is how his doctrine of Maya is often construed. This again happens to be a distortion of his message. Sankara looked upon Maya as the power of divinity, as something wonderful, as something which is both real and unreal. Sankara, therefore, never dismissed the world as a phantasmagoria or chimera as claimed by some of his critics.

6.   This book represents an abridged version of my more comprehensive book on Advaitism entitled 'Sankara: the Founder of Hinduism'. This book will come out in New Delhi shortly.

7.   It is my sincere hope that this book will enable all those who are seriously interested in Indian philosophy to grasp basic features of Sankara's Advaitism. Nobody can deny that Advaitism occupies a pre-eminent place in the edifice of Indian metaphysical thought.

8.   Finally, I will like to thank my local Secretary Miss Melanie Basdeo for typing the manuscript of this book with great diligence. Moreover, entire credit for the lay out of the book is due to her. I will also like to express my appreciation of Mrs. Sushmita Bhuyan for proof-reading the manuscript with every care.

****

PREFACE

The Advaita or non-dual school of thought stands at the centre of India's philosophical tradition, and, Bhagavatpada Adi Sankaracarya, the principal exponent of Advaita is the most illustrious of Indian thinkers. It is hard to think of a parallel to Sankara in any of the philosophical systems of the world. Maybe if one were to put together Plato, Aristotle, Acquinas, Hegel, Kant and Heidegger in one personality it would be possible to have someone approaching the importance of Sankara.

Advaita *darshana* is indeed highly scholastic and intellectually challenging. To understand Advaita requires considerable discipleship and to write a book on it is certainly even more daunting. It would not be so difficult if one were writing for one's peers but to seek to simplify the system for a general readership is something few would have courage to contemplate and undertake. Yet this is exactly what Dr. Prakash Joshi, India's High Commissioner to Guyana has done in this remarkable little book *Advaitism Made Easy*. Only one who has the deepest understanding of the Advaita can think in terms of simplifying it for a general readership.

Dr. Joshi is no new comer to expounding India's religious, theological, and philosophical traditions. He is the author of an impressive two-volume work, *Saga on Hinduism* and a large and more comprehensive work on Advaita is currently with publishers in India. In this regard he is ideally qualified to not only represent but also *re-present* India abroad. This ability to find the time in the midst of his ambassadorial duties to present the purest cultural achievement of India reminds one and continues in the tradition of Dr. Sarvapalli Radhakrishnan, India's modern philosopher, scholar, statesman and diplomat, *par excellence.*

Indian diplomatic and cultural missions abroad have been engaged in promoting the widely variegated aspects of culture: music, dance, yoga, language and so on. This is indeed laudable especially in such a country like Guyana where there is a large population of persons of Indian origin. Presenting India's principal philosophical tradition inestimably raises the level of this contribution

Though small in size Dr. Joshi has succeeded in capturing the gist of this great school of Indian philosophy and in this sense has done a great service in promoting the culture of India. But equally, if not more important, he has done a great service to the Guyanese public in writing *Advaitism Made Easy.*

Few Indian diplomats have sought to understand the Guyanese public as Dr. Joshi has done and few have come in contact with a larger cross-section of the Guyanese population as he. His constant visits to far off coastland villages have served to cement the bonds of friendship between India and Guyana, and to deepen the understanding and appreciation for India. More than anything else he has done his *Advaitism Made Easy* is his best attempt in this endeavor. It is his gift to the Guyanese people.

Swami Aksharananda.

"...as a prophet and as a thinker, Sankara stands among the greatest figures in the history of the world. He is primarily, the unrivalled propounder of Advaita Vedanta, the non-dualist aspect of the Vedic Teachings. By means of his remarkable clearness, his supreme wisdom, and his profound spirituality, he has so stamped himself upon Vedanta that it has remained the paragon of Indian Philosophy, and has given solace to the sorrowful hearts of a large segment of mankind."
[Christopher Isherwood.]

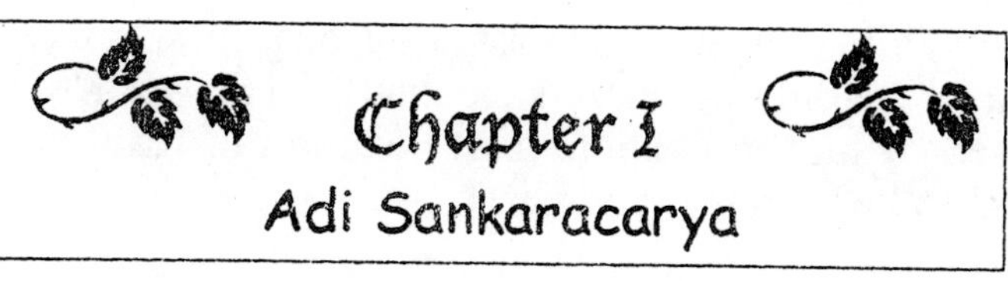

Chapter 1
Adi Sankaracarya

Though Adi Sankaracarya lived a brief life of only 32 years, he distinguished himself as a philosopher, as a poet as well as an indefatigable missionary. He strove to create a sense of unity among Hindus which was totally lacking until then. He rendered a signal service to Hinduism by his crusade against excesses of ritualism in which large segments of the worshippers had begun to indulge and as a result of which they were moving away from the true path of spirituality.

Sankara first and foremost is known as the "Founder of Advaitism". Though heavily influenced by the Upanisads and the Gita, Advaitism stands apart as a distinct theology in its own right by its coherence, impeccable logic, explicit postulates, and, most important, by its clear-cut conclusions. These features were generally lacking in earlier scriptures.

To Sankara our world did not represent the ultimate Reality. This is because everything we observe in it is marked by impermanence and change; it exists only for a limited period of time. It cannot, therefore, represent the ultimate truth.

Following such reasoning, Sankara concludes that the ever-changing observable universe around us is in some way unreal. This is how Sankara's famous doctrine of Maya originated.

While Sankara no doubt described the world around us as 'Maya', he did not deny its existence. The word 'Maya' was not used by him to connote total negation of reality. He held 'Maya' to be both real and unreal.

Sankara divided reality into two parts - higher and lower. He used the terms *"Paramarthika"* (transcendent) and *"Vyavaharika"* (practical) for categorization of the Absolute.

The phenomenal world around us marked by diversity and flux was deemed by him to be true only at the level of Vyavaharika (Practical) reality. Behind it lies the transcendent reality (Paramarthika) which epitomizes the absolute truth.

Sankara has waxed eloquent while portraying this transcendent reality. What is its nature? Sankara repeatedly affirms that it is beyond description, beyond the ken of human knowledge. It is something which human mind can never grasp. Brahman is attributeless. It is beyond names, beyond categorization, beyond the limitations of time and space, beyond change. It is eternal, unborn, and immutable; It is One without a second, and when man cognizes this fact, there is nothing more left for him to know or understand. The essential nature of Brahman is Absolute Truth, Absolute Existence and Absolute Bliss.

But if there is nothing but Brahman, then what about the genesis of the world? How did the world come into being?

Is it same or distinct from the Creator? Was there a Creator behind the world, and, if so, what are His attributes?

As we shall see in the next chapter, Hindu scriptures and various schools of philosophy like Samkhya, Yoga, etc. give divergent answers to these questions. Sankara once for all put an end to this controversy by laying down that everything is Brahman and there is nothing else apart from it. There has been therefore no creation of the world in the real sense and its existence cannot be attributed to any Creator.

In the same way, Sankara dealt with another major issue which had divided Hindu metaphysics, namely, the relationship between the Soul and Brahman. Sankara unambiguously affirmed the absolute identity between the two. One finds that he invariably portrayed the Soul in terms identical with those used to describe Brahman.

Thus, the basic tenets of Sankara's Advaitism can be said to be the sole reality of attributeless Brahman, Its essential non-difference from the world and identification of Atman with Brahman. This is admirably summed up in following aphorism of Sankara: "Brahman alone is real, the material world is illusory and Jiva is identical with Brahman". Finally, salvation is defined as acquisition of supreme knowledge. When this state is reached, all the artificial distinctions wither away, and man realizes what he truly is i.e. Brahman.

This in essence is Sankara's Advaitism. It is breathtaking in its generalization, dazzling in its grandeur and unimpeachable in terms of its logical argumentation. Another distinguishing feature of Advaitism is its total lack of ambivalence. It is these facets of Advaitism which put it on a pedestal and set it apart from other theologies. No wonder, Sankara's metaphysics has received glowing tributes from scholars, both Indian and foreign, in modern times as well as ancient.

Sankara did not introduce any major new doctrine into Hinduism, barring his explicit formulation of the doctrine of Maya. He took the scriptures, especially the Upanisads, as the foundation of his theology. But Sankara's greatness lies in the fact that he formulated a system of metaphysics free from internal inconsistencies. He construed in a uniform way the Upanisads, the Gita and the Brahma-Sutras, and this is why he is lauded to this day as a metaphysician par excellence.

But Sankara was not a dry intellectual, merely engaged in profound speculation about the nature of the Absolute. He was also a mystic and fully vouched through his own transcendental experiences for the truth of the basic Advaitic dogma that Brahman is the sole reality and is non-distinguishable from the Soul.

Sankara was also an ardent devotee. He composed voluminous poetry suffused with love of God. Sankara in no way repudiated idolatry. In fact, he used to pray in temples regularly, and many temples owe their origin to his inspiration. Prior to Sankara's times, a number of schools of philosophy had come into prominence which rejected the authority of the Vedanta. Buddhism, in particular, had rapidly spread, making deep inroads into Hinduism. Sankara highlighted in his writings the lacunae in other schools of theology then in vogue. He engaged in numerous polemics with Buddhist monks and brought home to them the imperfections in their systems of thought.

Contrary to popular belief, Sankara did not advocate

forsaking of worldly life by one and all. He himself remained active throughout his life, meeting people, preaching to them and guiding them towards the appropriate modes of worldly conduct.

While he repeatedly affirmed the existence of the transcendent Brahman, which he looked upon as the sole Reality, he never decried the worldly life. He considered due performance of one's actions as a means of self-purification, as a pathway to salvation. This is why he exhorted people to lead simple, pure lives marked by compassion and love towards all. Contrary to what some believe, Sankara attached highest importance to observance of ethical norms in daily life. To argue that Sankara held morality and immorality on the same par as they both belonged to the (unreal) realm of Maya is to do grave injustice to him and to totally misconstrue his message.

By the time Sankara emerged on the scene, idolatry had become wide-spread, and Vedic rites based on offering oblations to fire were no more in vogue. People used to worship images of different deities little realizing that they were a manifestation of the same God. Sankara initiated the custom of simultaneously praying before idols of five deities, thus emphasizing that various idols basically represented the same Supreme Being. He once argued that Vishnu and Siva were one and the same. This was almost a sacrilegious idea those days when Vishnu and Siva were looked upon by their followers as not only totally different, but mutually antagonistic. Sankara thus fostered the concept of unity of godhead and linked it to idolatry. He was also able to cleanse idolatry of various superstitions and other undesirable practices with which it had become associated.

If there was one area in which Sankara was truly a pioneer and in which he made a complete break with the savants who preceded him, it was in his role as an evangelist. Sankara set up four monasteries in four corners of India. They were meant for habitation of monks who had embraced the path of harsh monasticism. These monks were required to preach to the people living in areas contiguous to their monastery and thus propagate the true message of Advaitism. Hinduism never had a permanent cadre of itinerant evangelist monks as created by Sankara and herein lies his greatness.

Until the advent of Sankara, there was no notion of "Hinduism" as constituting one religion. People worshipped different deities blissfully ignorant of the underlying unity. Devotees of Vishnu and Siva considered themselves as poles apart from each other, and there was no love lost between them.

Sankara was the first sage who made a conscious attempt to create a sense of unity among Hindus. He showed how the main scriptures of Hinduism could be construed in a uniform and consistent way. Moreover, he also demonstrated how metaphysical doctrines, ritualism and norms of ethical conduct for daily living could be harmoniously blended together within the framework of Advaitism. No other savant prior to Sankara had even made an attempt in this direction. By establishing monasteries in four corners of India, Sankara gave a concrete and tangible proof of how Hindus, no matter living in what part of India, constituted one community, one people, who were bound to each other by shared spiritual and ethical values.

This is why the author feels amply justified in giving

the appellation 'Founder of Hinduism' to Sankara in this publication.

"I bow my head before Sri Sankara, the preceptor of the humble disciples who are renowned for their knowledge of the bhasya and who drink the nectar flowing from the bhasya-lotus which owes its origin to the mamasa-lake of Sri Sankara's mouth and who, like the bees, are eagerly lifting up their faces from all quarters."   [Padmapada]

"The great teaching which issues from the lotus-face of the Bhagavatpada, which has the non-dual Brahman as its primary import, which destroys phenomenal existence and which, while admitting of several interpretations by the (numerous) ancient preceptors, exists in all its grandeur, in the same way as the river Ganga which, issuing from the foot of Visnu, assumes different courses on reaching different lands."   [Appayya Diksita.]

Chapter 2
Sankara's life, work and achievements

Sankara was born towards the end of seventh century in a village called Kalati in Kerala in South India. His parents were highly pious Nambooodri Brahmins who were ardent devotees of Siva. His father as well as his grandfather ran a small Vedic school. Before Sankara's birth, Lord Siva had reportedly appeared in his father's dream and told him that he intended to take birth as his son.

Sankara gave proof of his prodigious memory from a very young age. He masters the Sanskrit alphabet when he was a mere toddler. He loses his father before he reaches the age of five. A little later Sankara vows to become a hermit when he was no more than eight years of age. This happens in following circumstances:

One morning while he was taking his morning bath in a river near his house a giant crocodile pounces on him and begins to drag him into the depths of water. Sankara is released only after he promises that he would renounce worldly life and become a wandering mendicant. He accordingly prepares to leave his home immediately. While bidding a tearful farewell to his mother, he assures her that he would return whenever she needed him. Sankara had great love and respect for his mother. Subsequently, when she passed away he cried inconsolably and performed her last rites, though he was debarred from doing so, as he was a

Sannyasi. All this illustrates Sankara's overflowing love for his mother and shows that Advaitism in no way rejects sentiments and emotions which ordinary people harbour towards their loved ones.

Sankara then travels northwards and meets his Guru Govinda. Sankara had profound reverence for Govinda whom he describes as a manifestation of the Absolute. This is how he portrays him in the very first verse of his major treatise on Advaitism, 'Vivekchoodamani'.

Sankara subsequently meets another renowned savant, Gaudapada, whom he venerated, looking upon him as his Guru's Guru. Gaudapada had earlier explicitly enunciated some of the key doctrines of Advaitism so much so that his philosophy can be regarded as precursor of what Sankara was to propound later. But Gaudapada also had marked inclination towards Buddhism. Since Sankara was influenced by him, a conclusion has been drawn by some scholars that Sankara too secretly harboured sympathies for Buddhism; some of them have gone to the extent of describing Sankara pejoratively as a "Crypto-Buddhist". The author has shown later on in this publication how such a surmise is totally unwarranted.

Sankara then comes to Kasi, where after an encounter with an untouchable, he is forced to admit that caste-based distinctions could not be reconciled with Advaitism. This is simply because according to Advaitism all human beings partake of the same essence and are therefore on the same par. It is in Kasi that he writes his famous commentaries on the Gita, the Upanisads and the Brahma-Sutras, which are regarded, and with every justification, as representing the acme of Hindu philosophy.

Sankara did not have many years to live after completion of this monumental task. He travelled extensively in India and establishes monasteries in its four corners, in Badrinath, in Puri, in Dwaraka and in Sringeri. These were meant for exclusive habitation of monks who had dedicated themselves to a life of study and contemplation. They were required to propagate the message of Advaitism among the people living in their vicinity. Sankara was the first Hindu sage who created a permanent cadre of evangelist monks in this manner..

Sankara, while being an ardent proponent of the doctrine of attributeless Brahman, was also a fervent devotee of Siva, Vishnu and other deities. He continuously affirmed that various gods were merely a projection of the same Absolute. He thus tried to bring together and create a sense of oneness among worshippers of different deities. He tried to bridge the chasm between Vaishnavites (followers of Vishnu) and Saivites (followers of Siva) by emphasizing that Siva and Vishnu represented the same God.

In a temple in Badrinath in North India, whose construction was blessed by him, he appointed a priest from Kerala to carry out the rituals; similarly, in a temple in South India, a priest from North was put in charge. This was clearly an attempt on Sankara's part to unify the Hindus, and to demonstrate that they belonged to one common religion, to one common faith.

Sankara urged priests to guide people towards

observance of the correct mode of conduct in their dealings with others. He attached utmost importance to righteousness in daily life. He exhorted people to be compassionate and loving towards each other. This was the essence of the system of ethics which he preached.

In Sankara's times, a number of schools of philosophy had emerged. Some of them superficially acknowledged the authority of the Vedas, but construed them in a most peculiar way. One such school which had grown in popularity was that of Mimamsakas. It held that the primary purpose of Vedas was to specify in minutest detail how various fire-based rituals were to be performed. The Mimamsakas looked upon rituals as a panacea for man's all ills and as a pathway to bliss, both in this life as well as hereafter. The Mimamsakas' system of metaphysics was so convoluted that even the "Supreme Being" was not given a particularly important status in it.

Sankara naturally rejected their basic credo that the primary purpose of Vedas was to lay down injunctions regarding the correct mode of carrying out rituals. He had long arguments with leading Mimamsakas of his day and brought home to them how their thinking was vitiated by some fundamental fallacies. So persuasive was he, that many of them subsequently became his close disciples and contributed significantly to propagation of Advaitism.

Sankara was a Karmayogi par excellence. While wedded to a life of asceticism, he never withdrew from the world, nor sequestered himself into seclusion. He worked ceaselessly for the spiritual upliftment of the common people. This was the raison de'tre behind the setting up of monasteries by him. While describing the empirical world as a Maya, he never dismissed it as of no import. He lost no opportunity to emphasize the importance of love and compassion in daily life.

As regards the period of Sankara's life, this is a matter which has given rise to much controversy. There is a general consensus that his life span was from 688 AD to 710 AD. But a number of scholars hold that it is not possible to specify the dates of Sankara's birth and death so precisely. They take the view that the only thing that can be said with certainty is that Sankara was not born before 650 AD, and that he did not live beyond 800 AD.

There is also a small group of Indian scholars who hold that Sankara preceded Christ. This viewpoint does not appear to be tenable for reasons which are explained in subsequent paragraphs.

Let us first see how the extreme limits for Sankara's life span (650 AD and 800 AD) have been fixed.

The lower limit for Sankara's birth (650 AD) has been calculated on the basis of references in Sankara's writings to some savants whose life spans have been determined independently.   It is well established that Sankara was preceded by Gaudapada. One also finds allusions in Sankara's writings to Bhatrihari, a well-known philosopher. There is a degree of certainty as to which period Gaudapada and Bhatrihari belonged. Since Sankara came after them, the possibility of Sankara's birth having taken place prior to their times can obviously be ruled out, and this is how the figure of 650 AD has been arrived at.

There is also much other evidence which substantiates this conclusion. Sankara wrote in elegant modern Sanskrit which came into vogue around fourth/fifth century AD. He was well acquainted with various schools of Buddhism; but these had emerged only in 2/3rd century AD. All this clearly precludes the possibility that Sankara was born prior to or immediately after the dawn of the Christian era.

As regards the conclusion that Sankara did not live beyond 800 AD, this is derived as follows. Sankara's works have been commented upon in texts whose period has been estimated as being around 800 AD. Obviously, Sankara lived prior to their compilation and hence the conclusion that Sankara could not have lived beyond 800 AD becomes inescapable.

The contention of some Indian scholars that Sankara was born in the pre-Christian era is based on the following.

They adduce the evidence of genealogical records which are extant in some of the monasteries set up by Sankara. These purportedly show that the above monasteries were established before the dawn of Christianity. Similarly, it is pointed out that Sankara's name is mentioned in various Puranas which were compiled around the beginning of the Christian era. Hence it is argued that Sankara must have preceded Christ.

But it is easy to refute these arguments. The authenticity of the genealogical records in various monasteries is very much open to doubt. As regards the allusions to Sankara in Puranas, not much weightage need be given to them. This is simply because these texts were substantially modified subsequent to their compilation.

Finally, to review Sankara's most important written works. Sankara is said to have authored more than four hundred texts, though his authorship of some of them is deemed dubious. But his major works for which he is justly famous are as follows: metaphysical treatises like Vivekchoodamani, Atma Bodh and Upadesa Sahasri; commentaries on the Gita, the Upanisads and Brahma-Sutras; and finally collections of devotional hymns as in 'Gita Govinda'. Special mention needs to be made here of Vivekchoodamani as well as his commentary on Brahma Sutras which is known as Sankara Bhashyam.

Vivekchoodamani contains a detailed exposition of Advaitism and the study of this text is a 'must' for any serious student of this theology. As regards Sankara Bhashyam, one comes across in it a wealth of information regarding various schools of philosophy which were prevalent during Sankara's times. Sankara Bhashyam therefore provides invaluable information regarding evolution of Hinduism as well as about the conflicting schools of philosophy which held sway around the dawn of the Christian era.

"The objects of sense in the world ever changing - These we adhere to as things of reality; But in the ocean of birth and death, they drown us. How long shall we wander in this path of dreams? This world to us indeed seems permanent and fixed, Yet after all, what is it but a road of dreams to which life after life we must perforce return?   [Seami Motokiyo.]

"A life devoted to the interests and enjoyments of this world, spent and wasted in the slavery of earthly desires, may be truly called a dream, as having all the shortness, vanity and delusion of a dream; only with this great difference, that when a dream is over nothing is lost but fictions and fancies; but when the dream of life is ended only by death, all that eternity is lost, for which we were brought into being." [William Law.]

Chapter 3

Ferment in early Hinduism and its lack of unitary Character

Hinduism is undoubtedly the oldest religion known to humanity. It was not founded by any single individual nor does it have a single authoritative scripture. Its origin can be traced to the ancient civilization of Mohenjodaro and Harappa which flourished around 3000.B.C. During this long span of time it far from remained a stagnant faith. It evolved and changed continuously as a result of which even its basic structure and message became a subject for speculation and surmise.

Around the dawn of the Christian era Hinduism encompassed a number of denominations that rejected Vedanta which is regarded as its very basis. There was no uniform interpretation of Upanisads, one of its most sacred texts. Hinduism thus lacked coherence and spoke in diverse, if not conflicting, voices. It is only against this background that one can appreciate the significance of Sankara's seminal achievement in unifying Hinduism and fusing together its disparate elements.

In what follows we have analysed how Hinduism evolved from earliest times until emergence of Sankara on the scene.

We start with Mohenjodaro and Harappa civilization which flourished around 3000 BC. Information about it is indeed scanty. But following can be said with a degree of certainty regarding the beliefs and religious practices of its inhabitants largely on the basis of archaeological excavations.

i] Those ancient people were iconolatrous.

ii] They worshipped a deity which shared many salient features with Siva like association with animals, asceticism, phallicism, and so on.

iii] They performed a ritual which bore resemblance to the rite of Puja in traditional Hinduism.

iv] They believed in the existence of Soul as well as in the Law of Transmigration.

v] They ascribed sanctity to certain trees and animals.

The Vedic Aryans, on the other hand, repudiated idol worship as well as phallicism. The concept of Soul was hardly developed in the Vedas and the Law of Transmigration finds no mention in them. Similarly, in these texts one does not come across any trees or animals as being deemed worthy of veneration by themselves, i.e. without being associated with any deity.

We thus see that the religious mores of non-Aryans were indeed sharply different from those of Aryans. Contrary to the popular belief, Hinduism has been much influenced by the beliefs and practices of non-Aryans. Hinduism acquired an amorphous character precisely because it derived its basic elements from two highly disparate sources, traditions and beliefs of Aryans and non-Aryans.   The core of Hinduism is normally associated with its three main scriptures, namely, the Vedas, the Upanisads and the Gita.   Let us now take a closer look at them.   We start with the Vedas.

Vedas are discursive in character and cover a wide range of themes which include everything from religion and rituals to history and magic.   The diversity of topics covered by them certainly detracts from their coherence.

But what is far more significant, the Vedas do not put forth any consistent system of metaphysical doctrines. Vedas call for worshipping of numerous deities.   But they describe individual deities one by one as pre-eminent so much so that all others are dwarfed before it.   Verses of this kind make us infer that the Vedas propound monotheism.   Thus, though the Vedas are superficially polytheistic, there is no doubt that their core reflects monotheism.

The Vedas again tend to be nebulous when it comes to visualization of their deities.   Vedic deities in many ways are deemed akin to man.   They are said to possess anthropomorphic attributes, both positive as well as negative. According to one Vedic conception, every entity in the universe, including men and gods, is endowed with a certain esoteric substance called 'Asu' which invests its possessor with admirable qualities.   Gods vastly surpass human beings in courage, strength, beauty, etc., only because they happen to be endowed with a much larger potion of Asu than man is.

While Vedas thus see a close analogue between man and god (or gods), they also make it clear that the deities belong to a plane altogether different from that of man.   Some of them are described as infinite in extent – a description which can never apply to man. These deities are occasionally depicted as being omnipotent, omniscient, etc., occasionally not. Thus, while the gods of the Vedas are anthropomorphized and are generally portrayed as having much in common with man, considerable ambiguity surrounds their precise characterization.

What is more significant one also comes across a clear formulation of the doctrine of monism in the Vedas. In a famous hymn called "Nasudiya Sukt" in the Rig Veda the Absolute is alluded to by the neuter pronoun 'It', and is portrayed in terms which are totally divorced from our temporal world. Such an Absolute could not possibly be the object of worship of man.

We can therefore say that the Absolute of the Vedas was often looked upon as 'Personal God', while occasionally It was also visualized in starkly impersonal terms.

Similarly, the Vedas enunciate differing theories when it comes to explaining the creation of the universe. In some places God is put forth as the creator while in some others the very process of creation has been held as a 'riddle'. It is also said that nothing can be known about that remote epoch when the genesis of the universe took place.

The Vedic seers thus had grasped that the nature of the Absolute and the mode of creation of the universe were profound mysteries. They made some tentative attempts to unravel them but far from succeeded in clearly formulating their ideas.

As regards ritualism, the significance attached to it sharply increases as one passes from the earliest Rig-Veda to the latter Brahmana texts. In Brahmana texts due performance of rituals is regarded as all-important while in the Rig-Veda no special sanctity is accorded to them. Thus, in the case of ritualism again the Vedas do not propound any single clear-cut doctrine.

Turning now to the Upanisads: these texts were written from 800 BC to 300 BC or so. Unlike the Vedas which cover a number of topics, both religious as well as non-religious, the Upanisads mainly focus on metaphysics. Moreover, the same metaphysical themes are discussed in various Upanisads. There is no progression of ideas, and conclusions reached in one Upanisad tend to be posed as queries in another.

The Upanisads basically expound the concept of attributeless Brahman. Monism thus forms their central plank. They affirm again and again the transcendence of Soul and Brahman.

The Upanisads leave unanswered a number of key metaphysical questions, among which one may specially mention:

i]   Nature of the relationship between Soul and Brahman

ii]   If Soul is immutable and actionless, how does it govern man's all actions, his thoughts, etc. and is looked upon as the very source of his life?

iii]   If man's life is determined by the inexorable

Law of Karma, has God no role to play in it?

iv]	What is the relationship between immutable Brahman and our changing phenomenal world?

Thus, the Upanisads leave many key metaphysical issues unanswered. In the same way Upanisads do not speak in one voice when it comes to ritualism or injunctions for day-to-day living. Though they mostly debunk ritualism, in some places they commend it too. Similarly, while they generally laud asceticism, they do not at the same time totally repudiate worldly life.

One can therefore say that the Upanisads do not enunciate any clear set of doctrines, whether pertaining to metaphysics, or rituals or norms for daily life. Moreover these texts were construed in different ways by sages in the post – Upanisadic era. Each savant sought and found in them endorsement of his own point of view.

The Vedas and the Upanisads in conjunction failed to provide a unified basis for Hinduism. This is because both of these scriptures suffered from lack of coherence and multiplicity of views. More importantly, there are major areas of discord between them. The Vedas mainly focus on anthropomorphized deities and attach much importance to ritualism. The Upanisads, on the other hand, mainly concentrate on impersonal Brahman, relegating rituals to background.

The third main scripture of Hinduism, the Gita, also did not succeed in creating a unified basis for Hinduism. The Gita does not enunciate any single set of doctrines in a consistent manner, whether in the metaphysical arena, or in the field of ethics similarly; it does not clearly lay down the ideal way of life for man. It commends three paths to salvation, Bhaktimarg, Karmamarg and Gyanamarg, and never clarifies which of these three paths it regards as most preferable. It speaks of Personal God as well as Impersonal. Its characterization of godhead, of the soul as well as of the relationship between the two, has been construed in starkly different terms. The Gita appears to uphold involvement in worldly life in some verses while in some others it strongly advocates monasticism.

The diversity of viewpoints existing within the fold of Hinduism was further accentuated by emergence of new schools of philosophy during the closing centuries of the pre-Christian era. Among the major schools of philosophy then in vogue, following may be mentioned:

i]   Carvakas
ii]   Ajivakas
iii]   Samkhyas.

Main doctrines and beliefs of these schools were as follows:

The Carvakas were materialists. They totally rejected the existence of God or any supernatural being. To them man was nothing more than his body. They denied the existence of Soul and held that death spelled the end of man's life and everything connected with it. Naturally, to adherents of this school sensual enjoyments meant everything. They saw no purpose in observance of ethical norms and claimed that every man should spend his life in pursuit of worldly pleasures, uninhibited by any moral constraints.

If Carvakas called for unfettered pursuit of sensual pleasures, the Ajivakas represented the other end of the spectrum; they espoused harsh monasticism and total severing of links with the material world. Ajivakas too did not believe in the existence of a Supreme Being. But they held that the only way in which man could uplift himself spiritually was through total renunciation of worldly life.

As regards the Samkhyas, the main elements of their philosophy can be described as follows. Samkhyaism believes in the existence of two primary elements, Prakriti and Purusha. Prakriti consists of three Gunas: Sattvic, Rajasic and Tamasic, which represent purity, activity and inertia respectively. The Gunas are incorporeal and beyond the ken of sensory perceptions. Prakriti is all-pervading, and in the beginning the Gunas are in a state of dynamic equilibrium. Prakriti lacks consciousness but is capable of evolution. Purusha, on the other hand, is immutable but possesses consciousness. Purusha acts as a catalyst to trigger the process of cosmic creation, and this is how Prakriti undergoes transformation and gives rise to animate and inanimate entities. It would be observed that Samkhyaism does not presuppose the existence of God and attempts to explain the genesis of the cosmos in rationalistic terms.

Purusha roughly corresponds to the soul. There are supposed to be an infinitude of them corresponding to multiplicity of souls. Though Purusha is inherently immutable, it falls into the delusion that it is the doer, that it is experiencing happiness, sorrow, etc. This delusion of Purusha is responsible for man's transmigration. When Purusha realizes its distinctness from Prakriti, man attains supreme knowledge which leads to salvation, i.e. he is not subject to any more births or deaths. Moreover, Samkhyaism looks upon observance of highest ethical norms as essential for reaching the state of salvation.

Samkhyaism differs from Upanisadic philosophy in one crucial respect. The latter holds that there exists only one Reality, one immanent principle, in the universe; it focuses on its delineation, its visualization. Samkhyaism, on the other hand, starts with the premise that the cosmos evolved from two primary unrelated entities, namely, Prakriti and Purusha. Moreover, there is no concept of God in this school.

But notwithstanding these differences, Samkhyaism also has many points of similarity with Upanisads. Both hold that the summun bonum of life lies in obtaining release from the cycle of birth and death. The principle of transmigration and the Law of Karma are embraced by both. Similarly, they agree that salvation could not be achieved without acquisition of supreme knowledge. In Samkhyaism this knowledge consists of recognition by Purusha of its own transcendence; according to Upanisads, it corresponds to realization by man of the nature of the Absolute. Finally, observance of ethical conduct is deemed in both the systems as a sine qua non for spiritual progress.

One can therefore safely conclude on the basis of the preceding that around the dawn of the Christian era there were indeed diverse currents of thought in Hinduism. There was no consensus on the basic metaphysical doctrines of Hinduism, nor on the role of ritualism in human life. While the Vedas regarded ritualism as all-important, it was decried by the Upanisads and other schools of philosophy. Again the question as to whether a man who remained engaged in worldly life could attain salvation was not resolved.

But while indeed the main scriptures of Hinduism and various schools of philosophy differed on many crucial points, they shared some fundamental dogmas; for example, the doctrine of salvation, including its visualization and the way of realizing it, was set forth more or less in same terms by various schools of philosophy including Vedanta. Hinduism thus definitely rested on a common substratum. But it needed the genius of Sankara to grasp and highlight this basic core of Hinduism.

Another major event which occurred around this time and which had a profound impact on Hinduism was the emergence and spread of Buddhism: Buddha was born around 6th century BC. He laid down in simple, clear terms the basic principles of Buddhism, including the precepts for daily living. Buddhism grew into a major religion of India during the period from third century BC to fifth century AD. A large number of Hindus embraced Buddhism during this period.   Several explanations have been proffered to account for this phenomenon.

According to some scholars, large segments of Hindus turned towards Buddhism because they were disenchanted with the priestly class which purportedly was putting undue emphasis on minutiae of ritualism and insisting on large-scale animal sacrifices. But this analysis is not free from lacunae.

There is no clinching evidence to establish that Brahmins indeed occupied such a dominant position in the society that they could compel ordinary people to perform rituals against their inclination.   Moreover, it is only in Buddhist and Jain texts that we find references to large-scale animal sacrifices.   Obviously it would not be in order to be guided unduly by the testimony of these text as they were not sympathetic to Hinduism.

There are other explanation too which account for the rapid expansion of Buddhism from 3rd century B.C to 5th century A.D.   During this period India was ruled by Mauryan and Kushan emperors who were Buddhists, and this no doubt contributed substantially to the spread of Buddhism. Moreover, many rich merchants had embraced Buddhism, and they made generous contributions to monasteries. This again gave an impetus to its propagation.

While Buddhism expanded at the expense of Hinduism, it also had a major impact on the evolution of metaphysical thought in India. Buddha had seriously challenged the doctrine that an omnipotent God had created this world. It was Buddha who for the first time had pointed out that the sufferings and tribulations of man could not be reconciled with the so-called existence of an omnipotent, compassionate Supreme Being. Significantly enough, the various schools of philosophy, which had emerged after Buddha during the closing centuries of the Christian era, did not postulate God's existence. It may be recalled that there was no concept of God in the three schools discussed earlier, namely, Carvakas, Ajivakas and Samkhyas.   This development is clearly attributable to the impact of Buddhism. Moreover, there were two other major schools of philosophy which had emerged in this epoch, namely, Nyaya-Vaisaisikism and Yoga, where again God is relegated into background.

Buddha had hinted that the world could not be regarded as wholly real. This was because it was always in a state of flux and what was impermanent could not be held as truly real. The famous Advaitic doctrine of Maya traces its origin to this formulation. Buddhism thus played its part in imparting to Hindu metaphysics an entirely new dimension.

Finally, turning to the evolution of Hinduism during early centuries of the Christian era: This era truly marked a turning point in the history of Hinduism. It was during this period that the Vedic pantheon began to be superseded by influx of new deities.

Significantly enough, many of these deities represented adaptations of gods which were worshipped by non-Aryans from the time of Mohenjodaro-Harappa civilization. This is best illustrated by Siva. He was initially worshipped by inhabitants of Mohenjodaro and Harappa. Vedic Aryans were definitely not worshippers of Siva. They repudiated with undisguised scorn phallicism associated with Him. But by the time we come to the Svetasvetara Upanisad, we find that Siva is visualized as a pre-eminent, benign deity. This clearly shows that the Aryans after some initial hesitation accepted the cult of Siva. This is how non-Aryan gods got incorporated in the Hindu pantheon. Another major development which took place in this era was the increasing popularity of idolatry. This practice which was unknown during the Vedic era became Hinduism's most prominent feature.

Hinduism thus was continuously undergoing transformation. New deities were replacing older ones, new modes of rituals (idol-worship) were superseding earlier ones (fire-worship), and so on.   All this was leading to further fragmentation of Hinduism and loss of its cohesion.

This was accompanied by composition of a large number of semi-sacred texts.   Gods, goddesses and other supernatural beings were described by them in almost anthropomorphic terms.   These texts with their emphasis on mythology fostered superstitions among common people and the basic core of Hinduism began to be diluted.

It would be readily observed that Hinduism prior to birth of Sankara indeed presented a disconcerting scenario. As far as the visualization of godhead was concerned, the entire gamut of viewpoints, from espousal of monism to looking upon an inanimate icon as the very symbol of the Supreme Being, formed a part of Hindu metaphysics. Idolatry was acquiring increasing popularity and superficial observance of rituals began to be considered as all-important. There was no consensus on the ideal way of life for man. It was argued by many that man should embrace monasticism and dedicate his life solely to contemplation and worship of God.   Proponents of this school looked upon the world as devoid of any real meaning.   There were again many others who challenged this viewpoint and commended worldly life, provided of course ethical norms were not transgressed. They contended that the worldly existence lived righteously also opened the portals to salvation.

Thus, when Sankara emerged on the scene, Hinduism comprised several disparate elements and hardly presented a unified appearance; its adherents who belonged to different sects and denomination never felt that they shared a common faith. There was no agreement as to the message of the main scriptures of Hinduism. It was Sankara who showed how within the framework of Advaitism they could be construed in a uniform way. He laid down in clear terms precepts for daily living, for ritualism. Sankara thus started the process of unifying Hinduism. This is why the author has given him the appellation 'Founder of Hinduism' in this publication.

There may be disagreement as to the extent to which Sankara succeeded in this task. But it is indisputable that it was Sankara who firmly implanted the notion in Hindu psyche that Hinduism was one single faith with common scriptures, with common modes of ritualism, and this was no mean achievement.

"Give up identification with your family, your clan, your name and station in life which are associated with your living body (which is really a corpse through with blood is coursing)...." [V.C. No: 298]

"Activity grows by the growth of vasana (desire, passions, etc.) and by the growth of activity the vasana also grows. For such a person, Samsara increases, there is no cessation." [V.C. No: 314]

Chapter 4
Main elements of Sankara's metaphysics

This chapter contains a succinct overview of Advaitism based on Sankara's famous text, Vivekchoodamani. Vivekchoodamani is a self-contained treatise and presupposes no previous knowledge of other schools philosophy or metaphysics. It is also lucidly written. This is why we have adopted it as the basic text in this chapter in preference to much better known Sankara Bhashyam for elucidating salient facets of Advaitism. Though Sankara Bhashyam cannot be challenged from the point of view of its profundity or comprehensiveness, it calls for considerable background knowledge of metaphysics.

However, it needs to be borne in mind that to comprehend Advaitism in all its aspects, the study of Vivekchoodamani alone is not enough. This is because Vivekchoodamani deals with Advaitism from a certain perspective. To properly grasp the complexity of Advaitism, one needs to study Vivekchoodamani in conjunction with Sankara's other major works, especially his commentaries on the Gita, the Upanisads and Brahma-Sutras. These have been analysed in subsequent chapters.

The essence of Advaitism can be summed up as follows:

Brahman is the only reality in the cosmos. Everything

else, including what we see, hear, etc., is marked by a degree of unreality. The empirical world appears to be different from Brahman (though in truth it is not so) due to Maya. When man is able to break the fetters of Maya, he is said to have achieved self-realization. This is a state when he experiences supreme bliss during which all the distinctions between himself and rest of the cosmos disappear. Brahman is immutable, ineffable and has no links with anything which human mind can cognize, conceive or imagine. It is characterized by *SAT* (Absolute Existence), *CHIT* (Absolute Knowledge) and *ANANDA* (Absolute Bliss). This is why Brahman is known as 'Satchitananda'. Brahman and Atman are indistinguishable.

It would be pertinent to explain here briefly as to why Sankara ascribed unreality to the world. Sankara fully endorsed the dogma of identity of cause and effect. This led him to conclude that if the temporal world indeed emanated from Brahman, then it should also be marked by immutability as the latter is. But we all know that this is not the case, and the world above all is characterized by flux and change. Hence he infers that the temporal world cannot be deemed to be real in the same sense as Brahman.

Unlike the Gita or the Upanisads, Vivekchoodamani right in the beginning lays down that the primary objective of man's life is to achieve salvation. Quoting from it:

> *"The man, who, having by some means obtained a human birth, with a male body and complete mastery of the Vedas, is foolish enough not to exert himself for self-liberation, verily commits suicide, for he kills himself by clinging to things unreal." (V.C. No. 4)*

> *"What greater fool is there than the man who having obtained a rare human body, and a masculine body too, neglects to achieve the real goal of his life?" (V.C. No. 5)*

But how is this goal to be reached? Unlike the Gita which lays down three distinct paths, Bhaktimarg, Gyanamarg and Karmamarg, for attaining salvation, Sankara posits in Vivekchoodamani that this end could be achieved only through Gyanamarg.

> *"Let people quote the scriptures and sacrifice to the Gods, let them perform rituals and worship the deities, but there is no liberation without the realization of one's identity with the Atman, no, not even in the life time of a hundred Brahmas put together." (V.C. No. 6)*

> *"Neither by Yoga, nor by Sankyha, nor by work, nor by learning, but by the realization of one's identity with Brahman is liberation possible, and by no other means." (V.C. No. 56)*

Sankara equates salvation with total bliss. Man then becomes totally oblivious of his worldly travails. Sankara says in Vivekchoodamani:

> *"Fear not, O learned one, there is no death for thee; there is a means of crossing this sea of relative existence; that very way by which sages have gone beyond it, I shall indicate to thee." (V.C. No. 43)*

"There is a sovereign means which puts an end to the fear of relative existence; through that thou wilt cross the sea of Samsara and attain the supreme bliss." (V.C. No. 44)

But why does salvation lead to bliss? This is elucidated as follows:

Attainment of salvation is tantamount to acquisition of supreme knowledge. Man then becomes capable of differentiating what is real from what is illusory. Man's sorrow arises because he clings to what is ephemeral and transient, believing in his ignorance that it would remain unchanged for eternity. But inevitably this does not happen, and he plunges into sorrow. Thus, it is due to man's ignorance that his sorrow arises.

Sankara illustrates this by using the metaphor of rope-and-snake which signify respectively the immutable Reality and the ephemeral world. A man in darkness gets frightened when he mistakes what is truly a rope for a snake. But his apprehensions disappear when light dawns and he realizes that the object in question was only a rope. Here darkness corresponds to ignorance while light connotes knowledge. This metaphor thus shed light on how an ignorant man gets perturbed by the happenings of our temporal world (the rope being mistaken for a snake in the darkness of ignorance), and how he becomes tranquil when he attains knowledge which makes him cognizant of the immutable, eternal Reality. (Realizing it was after all a rope in the light of knowledge.)

These notions are expressed by Sankara as follows in Vivekachoodamani:

> *"Identifying the Self with this non-Self-this is the bondage of man, which is due to his ignorance, and brings in its train the miseries of birth and death. It is through this that one considers this evanescent body as real, and identifying oneself with it, nourishes it, bathes it, by which he becomes bound as the caterpillar by the threads of its cocoon."* (V.C. No. 137)

> *"One who is overpowered by ignorance mistakes a thing for what it is not: It is the absence of discrimination that causes one to mistake a snake for a rope, and great danger overtake him when he seizes it through that wrong notion. Hence, listen, my friend, it is the mistaking of transitory things as real that constitutes bondage."* (V.C. No. 138)

But what causes man's ignorance? What is it which debars him from perceiving the reality as it is? Advaitism affirms that it is Maya which prevents man from comprehending the ultimate reality of Brahman, One without a second. Maya generates man's ego which induces in. him a feeling of being distinct from others. He then identifies himself mistakenly with his body and deludes himself into believing that he is a separate entity. This is how man forgets his essential nature, namely, he is in essence identical with Brahman.

But what is Maya like? The visualization of Maya in

Advaitism is indeed unique and finds no parallel in the Gita or the Upanisads.

Most people identify Maya with ignorance and look upon it as an entity which prevents man from perceiving the Reality. But Sankara portrays it in an entirely different way. According to him, Maya has many attributes of divinity. He ascribes the creation of the world to it; he deems it as neither real nor unreal. It is an integral part of Brahman. It defies description. Let us see how he envisages it.

> *"Maya is called avyakta (unmanifested). It is the power of Paramesvara (God). It is beginningless avidya. It is compacted of three gunas. It is more than sum total of its effects and is to be inferred from them by the wise whose intellect functions in accord with sruti (scriptures). She gives birth to this entire world." (V.C. No. 110)*

> *"It is not sat (real), not asat (unreal), not both. It is not bhinna (different), not abhinna (not non- different), not both. It is not sanga (with parts), not ananga (without parts), not both. It is very wonderful and of a form which is inexpressible." (V.C. No. 111)*

> *"Know that all these, Maya and its effects, from the mahat upto the body are asat and of the nature of the anatman like a mirage." (V.C. No. 125)*

It would be thus observed that Sankara's visualization of

Maya is indeed complex.   The existence of our very world, which is deemed to be neither real nor unreal, is ascribed to it. The doctrine of Maya indubitably plays a pivotal role in Advaitism.

By invoking this doctrine, many questions left unanswered in the Upanisads and the Gita can be resolved (see Chapter lll).   Among such queries one may mention the following:

i) What is the relationship between immutable Brahman and the changing, ephemeral world?
ii) How could Brahman create the world, while at the same time remaining unchanged?
iii) If the world arises due to the labours of an all-merciful God, why is it full of sorrow and anguish?

These queries which prima facie seem intractable can be easily resolved within the framework of Advaitism.   The second question becomes inherently invalid as there is no creation in the real sense. This is because the world does not exist on the same ontological level as Brahman, the former being a creation of Maya. Hence the question of reconciling the immutability of Brahman with the ephemerality of the world does not arise at all. Similarly, the third query gets invalidated as Advaitism does not ascribe the genesis of the cosmos to an all-merciful God.   There is no question therefore of blaming God for world's ills.

Finally, the baffling first question yields an easy solution by invoking the doctrine of Maya and this goes as: the world in essence is no different from Brahman; it is thanks to

Maya that Brahman's real intrinsic nature is veiled and it appears deceptively like our changing world. How Maya transforms Brahman which is undifferentiated, partless and immutable into our phenomenal world marked by plurality and change is something which human mind cannot grasp. This is simply because Maya is ineffable and totally beyond the ken of human cognition. Advaitism also answers this query by saying that there are two levels of reality: Paramarthika (Ultimate) and Vyavaharika (Practical). At the ultimate level of reality there is only Brahman while at the practical level of reality there is our world. It is the ineffable Maya which links these two levels of reality.

Turning now to the portrayal of Brahman in Advaitism: Unlike the Upanisads and the Gita where the Absolute is described in various, and sometimes sharply different, ways, Sankara invariably depicts Brahman in an identical manner. Brahman in Advaitism is always deemed as an epitome of Existence, Knowledge and Bliss. Moreover, it is always delineated as perfect, without parts, beginningless, totally beyond the ken of words, cognition and even conceptualization. We cite below some verses from Vivekchoodamani which show how Sankara portrayed Brahman in a uniform way.

> *"Therefore, the Supreme Brahman is the real; without a second; compacted of pure intelligence; free from defect; serene; without beginning and end; actionless; of the nature of unremitting bliss; free from all differences wrought by Maya; permanent; unchanging; pure; beyond the faculty of reasoning; formless; subtle, without name; immutable; such an effulgent Brahman shines."*

"The wise know it to be devoid of the tracheotomy of the knower, knowledge and the known; limitless; without variety; as pure infinite intelligence; as the supreme Truth."

"It can neither be thrown away nor taken up; it is beyond mind and speech, immeasurable, without beginning or end; it is Brahman which is superlatively full, the Light of all lights."
(V.C. No. 239-242)

On the other hand, in the Upanisads Brahman gets depicted in differing ways as illustrated by following two hymns.

"From Brahman gods, angels, men, cattle, birds, living fires, rice, barley, austerity, faith, truth, continence, law." *(Munduk Upanisad).*

Yajnyawalkya said:

"The saints call it the Root. It is neither big nor little, neither long nor short, neither burning like fire nor flowing like water, without shadow, without darkness, without wind, without air, without attachment, without touch, taste, sight, smell, without hearing, speaking, thinking; without breath, without face, without energy, without measure, without inside or outside; it consumes nothing, nothing consumes it."
(From Brahad - Aranyaka Upanisad).

In the first hymn Brahman is very much associated with the temporal world, while in the second it is totally divorced from it. This lack of consistency in Upanisads over delineation of Brahman arises due to one basic reason - these texts are ambiguous as to how genesis of the cosmos took place. In some Upanisadic verses Brahman is linked to its creation while in some others it is not, and this naturally leads to Brahman being described in sharply differing ways. Since in Advaitism there is no such ambiguity, Brahman could always be portrayed in a uniform way.

Turning now to Soul: as in the case of Brahman, It is always portrayed in the same way in Advaitism. Some of the hymns describing It are as follows:

> *"It (the atman) is not born; It does not die; It does not grow or decline; It does not change. It is eternal. Even if this body is destroyed, It does not become extinct even as space does not become extinct on the destruction of the pot which enclosed It." (V.C. No. 136)*

> *"The atman is unattached, actionless and formless. Without delusion there can be no connection of It with the world even as blueness has no connection with the sky." (V.C. No. 197)*

On the other hand in the Gita and the Upanisads the Soul (like the Brahman) is described in different ways. This is how Advaitism (where Soul and Brahman are portrayed uniformly) differs from earlier scriptures.

Here one comes across a paradox. If Soul is beyond the ken of the physical world, how does it control everything that man does, including even what he thinks and imagines? This paradox is not even addressed to by the Gita, while Sankara has no difficulty in unraveling it. Our world of action and change is not wholly real since it arises out of Maya. Therefore, it is wrong to regard actionless Soul and our empirical world as being on the same par. The Soul is linked with man, or with the world, through Maya whose mode of operation is totally beyond the pale of human cognition. There is therefore no contradiction involved in regarding the actionless Soul as the Seer of man.

As regards the relationship between Soul and Brahman, the Gita and the Upanisads do not come forth with a clear-cut formulation. On the other hand, Advaitism is explicit in this matter and affirms the identity between the two.

> *"Of Brahman and Atman (Soul) thus indicated by the words Tat and Tvam and whose meanings have been thus examined and determined, the oneness alone is repeatedly well established by the Sruti - Tattvamasi."* *(V.C. No. 243).*

Turning now to Advaitism's visualization of salvation:

Sankara portrays salvation in highly evocative terms as a state which is marked by bliss and bliss alone. It is reached when supreme knowledge dawns upon man. He at that time perceives that he is no more encapsulated in his tiny body, and that he has become a part of the unbounded cosmos. He cannot differentiate himself from rest of the universe. This is a state which defies understanding and is totally ineffable. Sankara depicts it as follows in Vivekchoodamani:

> *"Where has this universe gone? By whom has it been taken away? Where has it merged? It was seen by me just now; or; wasn't? What a wonder!"* (V.C. No. 484)

> *"What is to be discarded or what is to be accepted and what is different or what is distinct in the great ocean filled with the nectar of infinite bliss?"* (V.C. No. 485)

> *"I do not see anything here; I hear nothing; I do not know anything. I simply abide as distinct in the form of my atman in continued enjoyment of bliss."* (V.C. No. 486)

This is why Advaitism looks upon attainment of salvation which spells eternal bliss as the supreme goal of human life. But how is this state to be reached?

Achievement of salvation is tantamount to enlightenment which implies liquidation of Maya. But as explained earlier, emancipation from Maya calls for extirpation of ego. But ego is linked to one's awareness of possessing a separate body. Destruction of ego therefore presupposes total indifference to one's worldly existence, including even the basic bodily comforts. This is why Sankara exhorts the true spiritual aspirant to treat his body as if it belonged to somebody else and to inculcate an attitude of extreme distaste towards sensual pleasures. Obviously such a course of life would be feasibly only if one has embraced monasticism.

Quoting from Vivekchoodamani:

> *"A sense-object is more virulent than the poison of a king cobra. The latter kills only him who swallows it; the former brings about the death of him who merely looks at it."* (V.C. No. 79)

> *"Abandoning far away like a candala (outcast) the body full of excreta and flesh, and born of impure excretions of the mother and the father, become Brahman and attain your life-purpose."* (V.C. No. 288)

> *"Give up identification with your family, your clan, your name and station in life which are associated with your living body (which is really a corpse through which blood is coursing)......."* (V.C. No. 298)

A spiritual aspirant traversing on this path is required to desist from all worldly activities, including even those which are exclusively for the good of others. This is because any activity, however noble, imparts a feeling of "doership" to the individual, strengthens his ego and thus militates against his search for salvation.

> *"Activity grows by the growth of vasana (desire, passion, etc.) and by the growth of activity the vasana also grows. For such a person, Samsara increases, there is no cessation."* (V.C. No. 314)

In view of the foregoing Sankara looked upon Gyanamarg which requires that man sever all his links with the external world as the sole avenue to salvation. He averred that neither Karmamarg nor Bhaktimarg would lead to this goal.

> *"Not by yoga, not by Samkhya, not by Karma, nor by Upasana is liberation achieved. It is by understanding of the oneness of Brahman and the atman. Not otherwise."* (V.C. No. 58)

Sankara laid greatest possible stress on meditation. According to him, salvation could be attained only through most focused and profound meditation. He affirmed that only when one reached the topmost pinnacle of supraconsciousness, one would attain communion with Brahman.

> *"The destruction of the Ahamkara which is well-entrenched cannot be effected quickly even by the learned except by those who are firm and unmoving in nirvikalpa samadhi. For, vasanas (passions, desires) are long-rooted or variously produced."* (V.C. No. 343)

> *"Reflection is hundred times superior to hearing; meditation is hundred thousand times superior to reflection; nirvikalpaka samadhi is infinitely superior."* (V.C. No. 365)

It may be mentioned here that unlike Advaitism, the Gita or the Upanisads do not look upon engaging in intense meditation as a sine qua non for attaining salvation. This constitutes another area of difference between Advaitism and these scriptures.

50

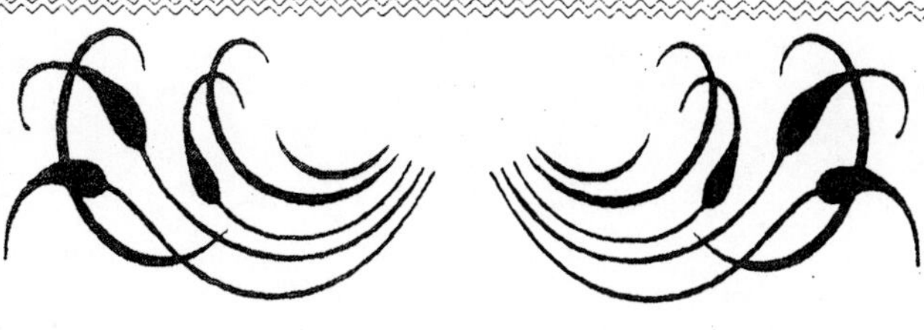

"Though I am unborn, of imperishable nature, and though I am the Lord of all beings, yet ruling over my own nature, I am born by my own Maya." [Sankara Bhashyam on Gita]

"This changeless, non-dual Brahman, in fact unborn, appears to undergo modification only on account of illusion or Maya and not de facto. For, if this change were real, the immortal Brahman would become mortal." [Karika 3.19]

Chapter 5

The doctrine of Mayavada: Its Genesis and Significance

The doctrine of Maya undoubtedly constitutes the central plank of Advaitism. This doctrine, which seemingly denies the very existence of our empirical world, is a source of great confusion and has been widely misconstrued. It has been claimed (fallaciously) that because Maya equates the phenomenal world with vacuity, it places ethical and unethical conduct on the same par. Such a viewpoint which does grave injustice to Advaitism can be put forth as follows:

1

> *"The ethical views of Sankara have been the subject of much criticism, and we may briefly consider the several charges. If all that exists is Brahman, and if the world of plurality is a shadow, there cannot be any real distinction between good and evil. If the world is a shadow, sin is less than a shadow. Why should not a man play with sin and enjoy a crime, since they are only shadows? What shall it profit us if we fight wild beasts and sacrifice our interests in seeking virtue in this dream of life?"*

Of course, the above argument is totally untenable and

represents a travesty of Advaitism. It has been adduced merely to illustrate how in some circles Advaitism was grossly misunderstood. This happened largely because many of Sankara's critics failed to properly grasp his visualization of Maya.

It should be evident to the reader by now that the doctrine of Maya not only forms the centerpiece of Advaitism, but also its most distinguishing facet. Sankara's visualization of Maya is indeed unique, and finds no parallel in any other school of philosophy.

Sankara envisaged Maya as both real and unreal, as ineffable, as the divine power of God. He never considered it as an illusion or devoid of import. It need hardly be emphasized that one cannot understand Advaitism unless one has grasped properly the doctrine of Maya. In this chapter following aspects of it have been focused upon:

i) Do the scriptures propound the doctrine of Maya?

ii) Can Sankara be regarded as the progenitor of this doctrine?

iii) How did Sankara portray the temporal world?

iv) Why is the doctrine of Maya regarded as so significant?

v) Was this doctrine generally endorsed by savants in the post-Sankara period and are there any points of ambiguity associated with it?

Let us take up these queries serially, beginning with the first one.

The term 'Maya" does occur a few times in the Vedas, the Upanisads and the Gita. But it is generally used to convey God's occult powers, His creative potential, etc; it also carries the more conventional meaning of chicanery, deceit, etc. It is rarely employed in the Advaitic sense of creating the illusion of there being a multi-faceted world, when in truth there is only Brahman.

Let us first analyse the usage of this term in the Vedas. In these texts Maya signifies the esoteric power of deities and their magical attributes. The Vedic seers never associated any unreality with the temporal world. There was no question therefore of their using the word Maya to impute unreality to it. Quoting from a Vedic scholar:

2

"According to H. D. Griswold the term 'Maya' has been used at least four times concerning Varuna (RV.V. 85.5.6; VIII.41 3.8) in the sense of 'occult power' and magic wiles (VIII.41.8). In the same way term Maya occurs thirty times at least in 'Indra hymns."

Turning next to the Upanisads: The word Maya occurs in them only twenty-five times. In most of these texts it is in no way linked with illusoriness which is the primary meaning of Maya in Advaitism. However, in some later Upanisads, Maya does acquire such a connotation.

However, one should not infer that the doctrine of Maya is alien to Upanisads because the word 'Maya' occurs in them infrequently, and is not usually deployed in the Advaitic sense of illusoriness. In fact, a large number of key Upanisadic hymns cannot be properly understood except by invoking this doctrine. This will become clear in a later chapter in which Sankara's commentaries on the Upanisads have been analysed. Given below are instances of some such hymns which clearly ascribe, though implicitly, unreality to our cosmos

i)   From the unreal lead to the real.
From darkness lead to light. (Br. I iii. 28)

ii)   "Because when there is a difference, as it were, then one sees another."
But when to the knower of Brahman everything has become the self, then what should one see and through what." (Br. Iv. 5. 15)

iii)   He gets death after death who perceives here seeming diversity. (Br. Iv. 4 19)

It can therefore be argued that the Upanisads generally endorse this doctrine, though by implication. This is why a scholar says:

3

> *"The presence (or absence) of certain words in the extensive literature of the Upanisads is not, after all, a serious matter. To argue therefore as to the presence or otherwise of a particular doctrine is a procedure entirely ridiculous; for it finds, as Prof. Ranade significantly remarks, 'the existence of a doctrine like that of Maya in words rather than in idea.' In fact, the Upanisads suggest the doctrine of Maya most strongly in passages where the word Maya or avidya does not occur at all. It is the famous Vacarambhana text and the passage 'where is duality as it*

*were' (yatra hi dvaitam ivabhavati) etc., which
truly contain the seeds of the Maya doctrine."*

Finally, turning to the usage of the word Maya in the
Gita: Here again it is of infrequent occurrence and is deployed
no more than 40 times. Moreover, it is not employed in the
primary Advaitic sense of illusoriness, but connotes God's
creative power, veil of divinity, etc.

Quoting from a scholar:

4

*"Prof. T. G. Mainkar in his book " A
Comparative Study of the Commentaries on the
Bhagavadgita' p.7, mentions that 'Maya' may
be said to be power or Shakti of the Lord Krisna.
Then again, Mainkar denies that Bhagvadgita
teaches the doctrine of illusionism. According to
him, five clear passages, containing the term
'Maya' (IV:6; VII:15-15, 25; XVIII: 61) do not
even hint at the doctrine of illusionism."*

Turning to the Brahma-Sutras, in this highly important
scripture the word Maya occurs only once, and is used as a
synonym for 'dream:

It can therefore be concluded that in the Prasthan-Trayi
(the Upanisads, the Gita, and the Brahma-Sutras) the word
Maya occurs but infrequently, and is rarely deployed to
explicitly convey illusoriness. But at the same time it needs to
be borne in mind that many verses in these scriptures would
defy understanding outside the framework of Sankara's
Mayavada. As shall become clear from the analysis of

Sankara's commentaries on the Gita, the Upanisads, etc., in later chapters, this doctrine in a way forms the substratum of these scriptures, though this is hardly apparent.

Let us now take up the question of what possibly motivated Sankara to evolve this doctrine: he was very much concerned with the question of creation. Did it take place, and, if so, how? This conundrum did not unduly occupy the attention of Upanisadic seers, nor did the Gita focus on it. This is because the Upanisads were mainly concerned with visualization of the Absolute, while the primary preoccupation of the Gita was with laying down an ideal way of life for man.

The Gita mostly ascribes the creation of the world to a Supreme Being. The Upanisads too now and then put forth this viewpoint.

It was Buddha who in trenchant terms brought out the implausibility of such a line of thought. He argues that there was no way in which God's visualization as a Supreme, all-merciful Being could be reconciled with His purported creation of our highly imperfect world.

Buddha says:

5

> *"If the world had been made by Isvara, there should be no change nor destruction, there should be no such thing as sorrow or calamity, as right or wrong, seeing that all things, pure and impure, must come from him. If sorrow and joy, love and hate, which spring up in all conscious beings, be the work of Isvara, he*

himself must be capable of sorrow and joy, love and hatred, and if he has these, how can he be said to be perfect? If Isvara be the maker, and if beings have to submit silently to their maker's power, what would be the use of practising virtue? The doings of right and wrong would be the same, as all deeds are his making and must be the same with their maker. But if sorrow and suffering are attributed to another cause, then there would be something of which Isvara is not the cause. Why, then, should not all that exists be uncaused too?"

"Again, if Isavara be the maker, he acts either with or without a purpose. If he acts with a purpose, he cannot be said to be all perfect, for a purpose necessarily implies satisfaction of a want. If he acts without a purpose, he must be like the lunatic or suckling babe. Thus the idea of Isvara is proved false by rational argument, and all such contradictory assertions should be exposed."

Sankara was able to obviate this dichotomy once for all by repudiating the very possibility of creation. Advaitism holds that there has been no creation of the cosmos in the real sense. It considers the Brahman as the sole reality. It looks upon the world as a creation of Maya and hence the former cannot be held to be on par with Brahman. Imperfections of the world therefore do not sully the sublimity of Brahman.

Mayavada thus enabled Sankara to resolve the paradox

of reconciling the existence of our imperfect world with the existence of the Absolute which is totally free of any taint.

Let us turn to genesis of Mayavada.

One can perhaps look upon Buddha as one who first propounded this doctrine, though in a highly nebulous manner. How else could one explain the following two well-known statements attributed to him.

6

> *"This world, O Kaccana, generally, proceeds on a duality, on the 'It is' and the 'It is not'. But, O Kaccana, whoever perceives in truth and wisdom, how things originate in the world, in his eyes, there is no 'it is not'.... whoever, O Kaccana, perceives in truth and wisdom how things pass away in this world, in his eyes there is no 'it is'. Everything is-this is one extreme, O Kaccana. Everything is not is another extreme. The truth is in the middle."*

7

> *"Verily, I declare unto you, that within this very body, marked as it is, and only a fathom high, but conscious and endowed with mind, is the world, and the waxing thereof and the waning thereof and the way that leads to the passing away thereof."*

Subsequent to Buddha, four distinct schools emerged in Buddhism. Two of them (Realist) posited that the visible universe which we cognize was indeed there. But this was denied by the other two schools (Idealist) which held that the objects of perception were a chimera and nothing but a creation of our mind. A famous Buddhist philosopher of the Idealist Schools, Nagarjuna, spoke of two levels of reality: transcendental and empirical. The seeds of the doctrine of Maya were thus being sown.

There is no doubt therefore that Buddhist theologians had brought into vogue esoteric concepts like illusoriness of the empirical world, existence of two levels of reality, etc., which were later to become an integral part of Advaitism.

These ideas were further developed by Gaudapada, a Hindu savant, who was also much influenced by Idealist Schools of Buddhism. Gaudapada put forth cogent reasons to argue that the world was an illusion and ascribed its creation to Maya. These subsequently found a precise analogue in Advaitism. Gaudapada reached this conclusion on the basis of two-fold arguments as cited below:

First, he claimed that the immutable Brahman could never undergo any transformation and thus bring into existence the empirical world. He based this argument on the dogma of identity of cause and effect which had become a part of metaphysical thought in India long before his times. Creation thus was ruled out as an impossibility. But this necessarily meant that our world of sound and sight could not be real.

> *"The dualists contend that the ever unborn and the eternally changeless Atman undergoes a change. How could an entity which is itself changeless and immortal become mortal."*
> *(Karika 3. 21)*

Gaudapada also followed another line of thought to reach the same conclusion. According to him, only that entity could be described as "real" in the true sense which was ever unchanging, which remained ever the same. Since these criteria are not fulfilled by our empirical world, he had little difficulty in inferring that it lacked reality.

> *"That which is non-existent in the beginning and in the end, is necessarily non-existent in the intermediary stages also. The objects we see are illusions, still they are regarded as real." (Karika 4.31)*

Based on the foregoing analysis, Gaudapada could logically argue that it was only thanks to Maya that the world could come into existence. This is because he had totally ruled out the possibility of immutable Brahman being tranformed into our world.

> *"This changeless, non-dual Brahman, in fact unborn, appears to undergo modification only on account of illusion or Maya and not de facto. For, if this change were real, the immortal Brahman would become mortal." (Karika 3.19)*

However, it needs to be borne in mind that there is a crucial difference between visualization of Maya by Gaudapada and Sankara. To Gaudapada Maya was not different from illusion; on the other hand, to Sankara Maya stood for nothing less than the power of divinity. (See Chapter IV) This aspect is elaborated further in Chapter VII.

However, one can surely conclude from what has

preceded that Sankara's formulation of the Maya doctrine owed much to the work which was already done by philosophers who preceded him. No doubt Sankara's conceptualization of Maya was unique but many of its elements were clearly enunciated earlier.

Let us now turn to the third query posed earlier at the beginning of this chapter. This relates to portrayal of our world by Sankara.

Sankara never dismissed the world as a pure illusion because it was a manifestation of Brahman, the Sole Reality. He describes it as follows in Sankara Bhashyam:

8

> *"Name and form which constitute the seeds of the entire expanse of phenomenal existence, and which are conjured up by nescience are, as it were, non-different from the omniscient God and they are non-determinable as real or unreal...."*

Dr. Radhakrishnan expresses the same notion somewhat simply as follows:

9

> *"The whole empirical reality, with its names and forms, which can be defined neither as being nor as non-being, rests upon Avidya."*

In the first quotation Sankara identifies the world with God. Surely he could not have looked upon it as a phantom or a dream as is sometimes put forth.

Sankara's portrayal of the cosmos in Vivekchoodamani is also noteworthy. It goes as:

> " *An unbroken series of perceptions of Brahman is this universe; so in every respect it is nothing but Brahman. In all conditions see this with the vision of illumination and a serene mind. Is it ever possible that he who has eyes can see anything other than forms all around? So too, what is there to engage the intellect of a realised man, save Brahman?*" (V.C. 522)

Here Sankara asserts that the world is a projection of Brahman. He thus rejects in no uncertain terms the central dogma of the idealist school of Buddhism which holds that the objects of our perception are nothing but a creation of our mind. In fact, he derides in caustic terms those who hold such a view.

10

> "*As a matter of fact, such things as a pillar, a wall, a pot, a cloth, are perceived along with each act of cognition. And it cannot be that the very thing perceived is non-existent. How can a man's words be acceptable who while himself perceiving an external object through sense-contacts still says, "I do not perceive, and that object does not exist", just as much as a man while eating and himself experiencing the satisfaction arising from that act might say, "Neither do I eat, nor do I get any satisfaction?*"

Sankara urged the common man to remain engaged in his worldly duties and to discharge them as per scriptural injunctions. He deemed Karmayoga as mandatory for the common man (i.e. one who lacked enlightenment) since there was no other way in which purification of his mind could be assured.

> *"..... Similarly the duties of the different stages of life are needed not for the fruition of the result of knowledge, but for emergence of knowledge itself." (B. S. Bhasya, IV.26)*

> *"Worship consists of dedicating one's actions to God. This is how man becomes capable of gaining the supreme knowledge." (G.B.18.56)*

Surely, Sankara's advocacy of Karmamarg would have been logically untenable, if he had truly deemed the world as totally lacking in substantiality, or as nothing but a void.

No doubt, Sankara often described the world as unreal. But it needs to be borne in mind that the term 'unreal' as deployed by Sankara carried a special meaning. To Sankara reality was something which was eternal and immutable. Since the world does not have these characteristics, he deemed it as 'unreal'. Thus, when Sankara described the world as unreal, he in no way wished to imply that it was an illusion or a chimera.

This is why Sankara says in his commentary on Chandagya Upanisad:

> *"All this world of names and forms with its seat in Brahman is real and not apparitional. But if you say it is real by itself, it is an incorrect statement."*

Having thus reviewed how Sankara envisaged the world, let us turn to the fourth query posed earlier, namely, the significance of the Maya doctrine in Advaitism.

It is thanks to this doctrine that Sankara was able to give a uniform interpretation to the scriptures. We saw earlier how he was able to reconcile the existence of immutable Brahman with that of our temporal world marked by myriad imperfections by invoking Maya to act as a bridge between the two. It is only thanks to Maya that it can be ensured that the sublimity of Brahman is not detracted from by the imperfections of the world.

There are a number of verses in the Upanisads and the Gita which seem baffling unless one invokes this doctrine. To give some instances:

"All this is but Brahman." (Munduk ll. 2. ii)

"There is no difference whatever in It. (Br. V. 4. 19)

"That great birthless Self is undecaying, immortal, fearless and Brahman." (Br. iv. 4. 25)

It is thus affirmed that there exists only one immutable, immanent Reality. But then what happens to the world?

Similarly, in the Gita the Soul is described as the Seer of man but it is said to remain unaffected by man's actions. There are many such hymns in the scriptures which seem to defy understanding.

The basic paradox posed in these hymns as well as elsewhere in the Gita and Upanisads is as follows: on the one hand, the existence of an immutable Reality is posited. This is variously termed as Brahman, Soul, God, etc; on the other hand, the existence of our changing ephemeral world is also acknowledged. Moreover, it is stipulated that the latter never taints the former, though the former creates and upholds the latter.

How does one unravel this enigma which appears to be incapable of a rational explanation. Here the doctrine of Maya comes to our rescue. Sankara basically argues that the temporal world is not real in the same sense as Brahman, being a creation of Maya. The former is a superimposition on the latter. This is why happenings in this world do not tarnish the sublimity of Brahman.   This is illustrated by giving similes such as the blueness of the sky remaining unaffected by the dust in the atmosphere. We will come across these arguments again and again in subsequent chapters.

We now turn to the fifth and final query posed at the beginning, namely, whether savants in the post-Sankara period generally accepted the doctrine of Maya and whether there are any points of ambiguity associated with it.

The doctrine of Maya indeed proved very controversial in the post-Sankara period. It was rejected by many leading savants and sages. It came in for bitter criticism because it ascribed unreality to the world. According to many of Sankara's critics, the concept of unreality of our temporal world was totally alien to scriptures and holy texts of Hinduism. This is why Sankara derisively began to be called as

'Crypto-Buddhist' in view of the fact that the notion of unreality of the world is very much propounded by idealist schools of Buddhism. But ascribing such an imputation to Sankara was totally unjustified and this has been brought out in Chapter VII.

Moreover, Sankara also evoked opposition because he gave supremacy to attributeless Brahman and not to Vishnu or Siva whom most people regarded as the Paramount Being.

Bhaktimarg was destined to become a dominant facet of Hinduism in the centuries following Sankara's death and much devotional literature was written during this period. Moreover, during this era, many renowned saints were born who did much to popularize Bhaktimarg. Among them were Ramanuja and Madhava who criticized Sankara because he denied supremacy to Vishnu whom they looked upon as the Supreme Being.

Thanks to all these factors, Advaitism was far from universally accepted during the post-Sankara period.

Finally, turning to Sankara's formulation of the Maya doctrine: There is no doubt Sankara did not clarify many of its key facets. How does Maya operate? How can it veil self-effulgent Brahman? Is it a part of Brahman or not? Maya cannot be a part of Brahman as It is partless; Maya cannot be distinct from It as this will negate Brahman's non-dual character. When an individual gains enlightenment only his individual Maya is destroyed. But how could a transcendent entity like Maya be apportioned in this way, with a segment of It getting obliterated while the remainder remains unaffected?

The various lacunae in the Maya doctrine were cogently put forth by Ramanujacharya, a leading twelfth-century sage. Some of them as described by Dr. Lott have been cited below:

11

"In his seven-objections Ramanuja argued with some force that the monist's (Sankara's) concept of inherent Ignorance is quite unacceptable.

i. *It has no proper locus or basis, as either Brahman nor the soul can be in such a relationship with it, without radically distorting their true nature.*

ii. *On the monist's own reckoning Brahman is self-revealing consciousness, which cannot possible be obscured by any such negating entity as hypothetical Ignorance.*

iii. *To say that its nature is neither real nor unreal also raises problems. If it were real, clearly this world undermine the non-duelist position entirely. But if it were the unreal cause of an unreal world, this would in turn require some other false cause, and so on ad infinitum. To say that this inherent Ignorance is revealed by Brahman is equally impossible; for Brahman is eternal, and the result of his revealing such Ignorance would be eternal bondage.*

iv. *To call it 'indefinable' puts it outside the possibility of being inexperienced. For all experienced things are either real or unreal.*

v. *Its existence is not supported by any of the acceptable means of knowledge. Scripture does speak of a principle of delusion, but this is quite different from the monist's theory. Scripture's Maya simply means the wonderful, but real, world-creating power of Brahman.*

  vi. The ideal that it is knowledge of an absolutely unqualifiable Brahman that can immediately remove such Ignorance is equally impossible for reasons already listed."

1: *Indian Philosophy, Volume III. Dr. S. Radhakrishnan. Page 621.*

2: *Sankara's universal Philosophy of religion by Y. Masih. Munshiram Manoharlal Pvt. Ltd. Page 78*

3: *An introduction to Sankara's theory of knowledge by N.K. Devraja, Motilal Banarsidass. Page 78*

4: *Sankara's universal Philosophy of religion by Y. Masih. Munshiram Manoharlal Pvt. Ltd. Page 79*

5: *Indian Philosophy. S. Radhakrishnan. Oxford University Press, Page 457*

6: *Indian Philosophy S. Radhakrishnan. Volume I. Page 368*

7: *Ibid. Page 380*

8: *Translated by Swami Gambhinananda. Advaita Ashram. Calcutta. Pages 333 & 334*

9: *Indian Philosophy. S. Radhakrishnan. Vol. II. Page 586*

10: *Translated by Swami Gambhirananda. Advaita Ashram. Calcutta Pages 418 & 419*

11: *Vedantic Approaches to God. Library of Philosophy and Religion*

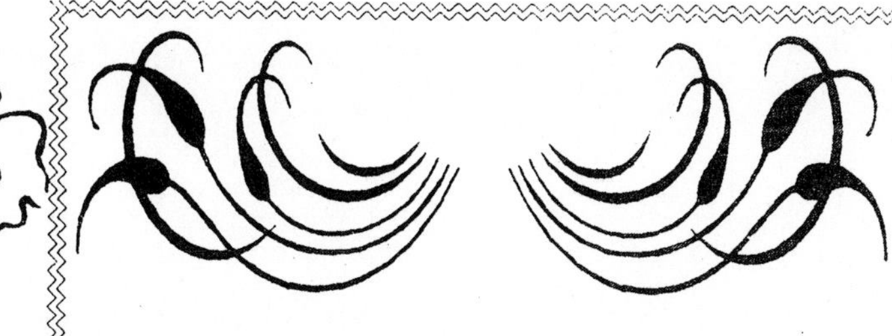

"O Great Lord of lords! Lord of all the gods! The destroyer of cupid! The destroyer of the city! The destroyer of the lord of death! O Hari! I am reflecting on you with all the devotion, repeating all these sacred names. Bless me, O merciful Lord." [Hymns of Sankara.]

"O Lord of the universe! My Lord! Lord of Gowri! Merciful to the surrendering soul! Conqueror of pangs of distress! The only kinsman for all! Salutations unto thee, salutations unto Thee, again salutations unto Thee." [Hymns of Sankara.]

Chapter 6

Brahman and Personal God : How does Advaitism reconcile them?

It is generally believed that the two primary visualizations of the Absolute in Hinduism, namely, Brahman and God, are mutually exclusive and antithetical. This is because Brahman, which is deemed to be totally delinked from our temporal world, cannot possibly be endowed with the qualities of love and mercy which constitute the quintessence of God. Hence it is concluded that Advaitism, which takes Brahman as its central plank, must be divorced from God as well as piety and faith which are essential for His worship. This makes us conclude that there is an essential dichotomy between monism and theism. This is why scholars say:

1

"It is generally said that Sankara's Advaita, though a masterpiece of intellect, cannot inspire religious piety. His Absolute cannot kindle passionate love and adoration in the soul. We cannot worship the Absolute whom no one hath seen or can see, who dwelleth in the light no man can approach unto."

2

"Sankara, as it has been said, gives us an Absolute, 'rigid and motionless' staring at us

73

with frozen eyes regardless of our selfless devotion and silent suffering. It is like 'a bloodless Absolute dark with the excess of light', 'blank which has every perfection except one small defect of being dead."

But, notwithstanding all this, Sankara had profound faith in God. He worshipped idols and many temples were built in fulfillment of his wishes. He composed numerous odes replete with devotional fervour.

A scholar, Y. Masih, says:

3

"If Sankara were not a committed theist, then he would not have composed a number of beautiful hymns. As a matter of fact he was a great theistic devotee. His hymns in Stotra Ratanvali and the most lyrical hymn Bhaja Govindam will easily place him among the great Bhaktas (devotees) of the world."

We thus see that monism and theism which appear prima facie irreconcilable were embraced simultaneously by Sankara. We have analysed in following paragraphs how Sankara could felicitously bridge the chasm between them within the basic parameters of Advaitism.

Let us first see how Sankara visualizes God. Sankara firmly believed that our cosmos was created by God and he saw no contradiction in associating our highly imperfect world with an all-merciful God. It may be recalled that long before Sankara, it was Buddha who had first put forth the

74

view that an almighty Being could not possibly be credited with the genesis of our world, whose hallmarks above all are sorrow and misery. (See Chapter V.) A prominent school of Hinduism, Samkhyaism, also embraced this dogma. But Sankara did not accept this reasoning and argued that God's omnipotence and imperfections of our world were not necessarily mutually exclusive.

Here we quote from his commentary on the Brahma-Sutras where he first adduces Buddha's argument (rejecting theism) and then goes on to demolish it.

4

> *"Opponent: God cannot reasonably be the cause of the world. Why?"*

> *"For that would lead to the possibility of partiality and cruelty. For it can be reasonably concluded that God has passion and hatred like some ignoble persons, for He creates an unjust world by making some, e.g. gods and others, experience happiness, some, e.g. animals, etc., experience extreme misery and some e.g. human beings, experience moderate happiness and sorrow."*

Sankara's rebuttal is as follows:-

> *"We say that these are merit and demerit. No fault attaches to God, since this unequal creation is brought about in conformity with the virtues and vices of the creatures that are about to be born. Rather, God is to be compared to rain. Just as rainfall is a common*

> *cause, for the growth of paddy, barley, etc., the special reasons for the differences of paddy, barley, etc., being the individual potential of the respective seeds, similarly God is the cause for the birth of gods, men and others while the individual fruits of works associated with the individual creatures are the uncommon causes for the creation of the differences among the gods, men and others."*

Sankara thus like a committed theist firmly asserted that God was very much there. He portrayed Him in another place as the creator, sustainer and destroyer of the cosmos - a portrayal with which any theist would readily concur. Quoting from Sankara Bhashyam:

5

> *"It was proved in the first Chapter that the omniscient Lord of all is the source of the origin of the universe, just as clay, gold, etc., are of pots, necklaces, etc., that by virtue of His being the ordainer of the created universe, like the magician of his magic, He is the cause of the continuance of the universe; that He is the cause of the withdrawal of the manifested universe; like the earth withdrawing* the four kinds of creatures."

Sankara wholly believed in the doctrine of incarnation. In his Bhashyam on the Gita he invariably portrays Krishna as incarnation in human form of the Supreme Being. He invokes the doctrine of Maya to account for this phenomenon i.e. of omnipresent God emerging in a human form. Sankara formulates and sheds light on this paradox i.e. (seeming) impossibility of reconciling immortality with mortality, as follows in his Bhashyam on the Gita:

6

"Arjuna might wonder how eternal God, who is above good and bad, who is above morality and immorality, could take birth?"

This is elucidated as given below:

"The whole world is controlled by my innate nature which is my Vaishnvi (divine) Maya composed of three Gunas. As a result, it (the world) remains ignorant of its own essence, i.e. Lord Himself. By subjugating Maya I appear as if possessing anthropomorphic features. I am not born in reality like rest of the world."

Sankara thus fully accepted the existence of Krishna, the Supreme Being, as man. Surely, nothing more could be demanded of any theist.

Sankara composed numerous devotional hymns expressing adoration of God and beseeching His grace. These hymns are polytheistic in orientation and eulogize various deities. He goes to the extent of extolling the bewitching beauty and charm of some goddesses. In his Bhashyam on the Gita Sankara totally endorses theistic sentiments of this text, its injunction to man to repose complete faith in God, and to dedicate his life to Him. Sankara looked upon Vedas as the fountain-head of Advaitism, though, as is well known, these texts abound with glorification of numerous anthropomorphized deities.   He never caviled   at such portrayals.

Sankara thus accepted the existence of God in all His manifestations.   He deemed God to be omnipotent, omniscient, etc.   He could envisage God as possessing anthropomorphic features and attributes.   He also agreed that God could be reached through His worship in iconic form.

Here following two queries come to one's mind:

i]   How did Sankara perceive no contradiction between omnipresence of God and idolatry?

ii]   How could a supreme rationalist like him portray God as an omnipotent, omniscient Being, while concomitantly investing Him with human features and attributes?

Sankara justified idolatry by arguing that God's presence could be more pronounced in some places than in others.   He says in Sankara Bhashyam:

7

"As for the predilection for His propitiation, consisting in visiting His temple etc., and so on, with exclusive devotion and for long, that also is not denied. For the contemplation of God is well in evidence in Vedas and Smritis."

8

"Even though the Supreme Lord transcends all limitation, still there can be a spatial limitation

78

for the sake of (His) manifestation. For the Supreme Lord does become manifest (in His majesty) out of favour for His worshippers. Or because He becomes specially manifest in particular spots like the heart..."

As regards the depiction of God both as omnipotent, omnipresent, etc., as well as being endowed with various human attributes, Sankara held that God allowed Himself to be visualized as possessing various human attributes in order to facilitate His worship by man, to enable him to focus on Him. Turning again to Sankara Bhashyam:

9

"But since God is the cause of everything, He is sometimes spoken of, for the sake of adoration as possessed of action, all (good) desires, all (good) smells, all (good) tastes" [Ch. III. xiv. 2], and so on. In the same way, there can be the mention of His golden beard. As the criticism that He cannot be God, since a residence is mentioned, we say, even for the one who is established in His own glory, there can be an instruction about some seat for the sake of adoration; for being all-pervasive like space, He can very well dwell inside everything. The mention of the limitation to His majesty also occurs with reference to the bodily and divine contexts for the sake of worship."

These quotations illustrate how Sankara reconciled God's omnipotence, omnipresence, etc. with his representation in an iconic form as well as justified investing Him with human attributes. He looked upon such visualizations of God as a means of facilitating His worship.

Finally, Sankara trenchantly repudiated some schools of philosophy like Samkhyaism and Nyaya-Vaisesikaism precisely because they were atheistic and essayed to explain the genesis and evolution of the world in rationalistic terms. Quoting from Sankara Bhashyam:

10

> *"Vedantin: with regard to this we say that if this has to be decided on the strength of analogy alone, then it is not seen in this world that any independent insentient thing that is not guided by some sentient can produce modifications to serve some special purpose of a man; for what is noticed in the world is that houses, palaces, beds, seats, recreation grounds, etc., are made by intelligent engineers and others at the proper time and in a way suitable for ensuring or avoiding comfort or discomfort. So how can the insentient Pradhana create this universe, which cannot even be mentally conceived of by the intelligent (i.e. skilful) and most far-famed architects...."*

It is clear from the above quotation that Sankara deemed creation of the world to be an impossibility without the intervention of a paramount, omniscient Being.

In view of the foregoing Sankara's credentials as a theist, as a devotee, seem impeccable. He accepted God's status as the paramount Being, thanks to whom the world comes into existence and is sustained. He had total faith in God and in his odes repeatedly exhorts man to seek His grace. These odes leave no doubt that Sankara looked upon God as a repository of everything that is noble and sublime as well as demonstrate unmistakably the ardency of his faith in Him.

Despite all this, there are two main reasons why a fundamental dichotomy is perceived to exist between Advaitism and theism. Firstly, according to Advaitism, there is no reality except that of Brahman which obviously means that in this theology God is not looked upon as the Supreme Being. But in theism it is the God who enjoys pre-eminence and none else. This is the reason why Advaitism is castigated for relegating God to a secondary status.

Dr. Lott, a scholar of theology, says:

11

"Whether described as lower-Brahman or as Lord (in Sankara's thought there is little difference between these two terms), a Personal Being endowed with glorious attributes is, even to Sankara, an unavoidable necessity."

"Nevertheless as serious theists they are at one in opposing the monistic view which only by way of concession ascribed a variety of personal qualities to Brahman: personal Brahman is a lower-order Being."

Another major reason due to which Advaitism and theism are deemed to be antithetical is as follows. Theism presupposes a clear-cut demarcation between man and God, between the worshipper and the object of worship. Advaitism admits of no such distinction as it identifies the individual self with the Supreme Self, or man with the Absolute. Advaitism's insistence that man in the ultimate sense is no different from the Absolute sharply conflicts with the basic postulate of theism which regards God as infinitely superior to man.

Quoting from Dr. Lott:

12

"To the theist, on the other hand, this whole method appeared blasphemous, not only because it 'robbed' the supreme Person of qualities essential to his being, but more specifically because it reduced his transcendent supremacy in relation to the individual self. It was just this divine supremacy that the theist experienced as the basis of worship, the highest end of man, and it was the knowledge of the self's dependence on this supremacy that he declared as the only means to ultimate liberation. On this issue the divergence between monism and theism is at most striking."

In other words, God and self occupy opposite ends of a spectrum in theism, but such differentiation is inadmissible in Advaitism. This is why one feels prima facie that worship of God cannot be reconciled with Advaitism.

Let us now examine how far the above-mentioned two reasons accounting for the purported chasm between Advaitism and theism are tenable.

Turning to the first theme, namely, the purported downgrading of God vis-a-vis Brahman in Advaitism. This, in fact, is a fallacious conclusion which reflects one's failure to properly grasp Advaitism's basic tenets. This would become clear from what follows:

Sankara looked upon the world as a creation of Maya; but God is inextricably linked with the latter. It may be recalled that Maya is deemed to be beyond comprehension. Its relation with Brahman can neither be understood nor delineated. In the same way we cannot determine the nature of the relationship between God and Brahman. They belong to different levels of Reality. This is why it is wrong to claim that Brahman is accorded a higher status vis-a-vis God in Advaitism. Terms like "lower" and "higher" which have relevance in our world carry no meaning when one comes to transcendent entities like Brahman and Maya.

Turning now to the second question: Who worships whom in Advaitism. It is true that in this theology the individual self is identified with Supreme Self. But this knowledge dawns only on a very rare individual who has been vouchsafed enlightenment. Most human beings remain shackled by Maya and regard themselves as distinct individuals, as separate from others, from the cosmos. According to Sankara, worship of God is very much justified, in fact enjoined upon, for all those who have not lost their sense of individuality, and obviously except a few enlightened souls everybody falls in this category.

Moreover, in this world of Maya as per Advaitism

God rules over the souls due to His infinite superiority over them. This is something which is fully in accord with theism. Quoting from Sankara Bhashyam:

13

> *"And within the domain of empirical existence, He (God) rules it over the selves which identify themselves with the (individual) intellects and are called creatures, and which though identical with Himself, conform, like the spaces in pots etc., to the assemblages of bodies and senses created by name and form that are called up by nescience.   Thus God's rulership, omniscience and omnipotence are contingent on the limiting adjuncts conjured up by nescience."*

We are now in a position to answer the question which we had posed in the beginning: was Sankara a theist? It is clear from what has preceded that this question has to be answered in the affirmative. Sankara's faith in God, in His sublimity, cannot possibly be doubted. His devotional poetry bears ample testimony to the ardency of his faith. Moreover, the fact that he regularly engaged in idol-worship effaces any lingering doubts that one might have about his endorsement of theism. While all this is true, Sankara's theism was subject to one crucial caveat. He held that God exists only as long as man considers himself as a separate individual. When this misapprehension is obliterated through acquisition of supreme knowledge, everything including God Himself seemingly disappears and merges into the Absolute.

Sankara believed in the supremacy of knowledge. But

how was it to be acquired? He considered reposing complete faith in God and engaging in ritualistic practices like idolatry as essential to reach this end. However, upon dawning of enlightenment, theism, which pre-supposes absolute belief in the existence of a Supreme Being, becomes irrelevant. This can be compared to a climber who needs a ladder to reach the peak, but the same ladder turns out to be superfluous once he arrives there.

1:      Dr. S Radhakrishnan. Indian Philosophy, Vol. II. Pages 648 - 649.

2:      As quoted in S. R. Bhatt studies in Ramanuja Vendanta. Heritage Publishers. Page 50.

3.   Michael Comans. The Method of Early Advaitic Vedanta Published by Motilal Banarsidass. Page 111.

4.   Sankara Bhashya. Translation by Swami Gambhirananda. Advaita Ashrama. 5, Delhi Entally Road. Calcutta. Pages 362 & 363

5.   Ibid. Page 299

6.   Gita Bhashya 4.6. Free translation by the author

7.   S. No. 5. Ibid. Page 440

8.   Ibid. Page 154

9.   Ibid Page 81

10.   Ibid. Pages 368 & 369

11.   Eric Lott Vedantic approaches to God. Library of Philosophy and Religion. Pages 121 & 122.

12.   Ibid. Page 121

13.   S. No. 5. Ibid. Page 334

"As the rope whose real nature, when not known is imagined in the dark to be a snake, a waterline, etc., so also the Atman is imagined in various ways."   [Karika 2.17]

"The Unreal cannot be born either really or through delusion. For, the son of a barren-woman is neither born de facto nor through delusion."   [Karika 3.28]

Chapter 7
Evolution of Advaitism from Gaudapada to Sankara

This chapter critically examines the impact of Gaudapada's philosophy on Advaitism. As already pointed out in Chapter V, Gaudapada had anticipated Sankara in formulating certain key components of the Maya doctrine. There is therefore a degree of overlapping between Advaitism and Gaudapada's philosophy. However, it needs to be borne in mind that there are also crucial differences between the two; for example, Advaitism has a grand, all-unifying character which is totally missing in Gaudapada's school of thought. But it is indubitable that Gaudapada's philosophy has almost a symbiotic relationship with Advaitism and, therefore, it is a must for any serious student of Sankara to familiarize himself with Gaudapada's works.

It is generally agreed that Gaudapada'a writings show a marked imprint of Buddhism. Sankara looked upon him as his Guru's Guru. This chapter aims to critically examine the extent to which Sankara can be deemed to be indebted to Gaudapada. This will enable us to assess how far Sankara's thinking was moulded by Buddhism which was a major source of inspiration for Gaudapada, and, more important, it will allow us to judge how far Sankara's critics were justified in giving him the none-too-flattering appellation of 'Crypto-Buddhist' in view of his linkage with Gaudapada.

We have for the sake of convenience dealt with this theme under following four heads:

i)   Points of analogue between Advaitism and Gaudapada's philosophy. This has been done on the basis of latter's main work, Karika, which is a commentary on the Mandukya Upanisad.

ii)   Crucial areas of discord between Sankara and Gaudapada.

iii)   Extent to which Gaudapada was influenced by idealist schools of Buddhism. It will be recalled that following Buddha two idealist schools emerged in Buddhism which regarded the world as lacking in reality. They looked upon it essentially as a projection of man's thoughts, ideas, etc. (See Chapter V.)

iv)   Finally, towards the end of this chapter, it has been brought out how a key metaphysical dogma put forth by Gaudapada and Sankara was enunciated by an ancient Buddhist text which predated them by a few centuries. Thus, a firm link between early Buddhism and the subsequent evolution of Hindu metaphysics, especially Advaitism, has been established.

Let us first review the extent of overlapping between Advaitism and Gaudapada's school of thought.

As pointed out in Chapter V, Gaudapada repudiated

the possibility of our world being created by Brahman. This is because he contended that what was eternal and immutable could never give rise to something which was ephemeral and changing. This naturally led him to conclude that our world was not real and its existence had to be attributed to Maya. Sankara too follows an identical approach to posit the unreality of the world and ascribes its genesis to Maya. (See Chapter IV.) This is undoubtedly a major point of commonality between Sankara and Gaudapada.

Secondly, Gaudapada affirms the identity between the Self or Soul and the Absolute. This is another key plank of Advaitism.

Quoting from Gaudapada's Karika:

> *"Since the identity of the (Jiva) and the Self (Atman) among themselves has been praised and the multiplicity is severely condemned in the scriptures, non-duality alone is rational and correct." (3.13)*

When man recognizes this identity between his Self and the Absolute, he is said to have attained enlightenment. But how is this sublime objective to be achieved? Gaudapada held that only the path of Knowledge and adherence to the rigid norms of monasticism would lead one to this pinnacle of spirituality. He rejects any role to rituals or devotional practices in achieving this end.

It may be recalled from Chapter IV that Sankara too considered the path of Knowledge as the sole conduit to enlightenment. He rejected with vehemence that mere carrying out of rituals or mere knowledge of scriptures would propel one towards this goal.

When it comes to portrayal of a Supreme Sage, both Gaudapada and Sankara are fully in accord. A supreme sage is described by Gaudapada as emancipated from the cycle of births and deaths, and as one who is firmly established on a pinnacle of tranquillity and bliss from which he never swerves away, whatever be the perturbations in the surrounding milieu.

One comes across vivid descriptions of such a sage in his Karika which go as follows:

> *"This highest bliss is based upon the rediscovery of the Self. It is peace identical with liberation, indescribable and unborn. It is further described as the omniscient Brahman for it is one with the unborn Self which is the object of the Knowledge-Absolute." (3.47)*

> *"When he has attained the state of Brahman, a state of complete non-duality which is beginning and end or a middle - what else remains for him to desire for?" (4.85)*

> *"The Realisation of Brahman is itself the humility natural to the Brahman. Their mental equipoise is also declared to be spontaneous. They are said to have attained perfect sense control - as it comes quite natural to them. He who thus realises the Brahman*

which is all peaceful, himself becomes tranquil and peaceful." (4.86)

It will be recalled from Chapter IV (see its end portion) that Sankara too portrays an enlightened sage in identical terms.

While Gaudapada asserted the existence of non-dual Reality as the ultimate truth, he did not deny that there was duality in temporal life. He admitted that there were far more passages in scriptures speaking of duality than repudiating it. He reconciles this paradox by pointing out that the doctrine of non-duality being very esoteric could be grasped only by the truly enlightened. Duelist passages in scriptures were accounted for by saying that they pertained to ritualism and were meant for edification of ordinary people.

Quoting from his Karika:

> *"The separateness of the Jiva and the Atman which has been declared in the ritualistic portion of the Veda, where it deals with the creation of the Universe, can only be figurative because this portion is a description anticipating what is to follow. This statement regarding a dualistic concept can never have any literal meaning."* (3.14)

> *"The Scriptural statements illustrated by the examples of earth, iron, sparts, etc, etc., regarding the notion of the world created or otherwise - can serve ultimately the purpose of explaining only the unity of the Individual-Self*

*with the Universe-Self. In fact multiplicity
does not exist at all." (3.15)*

*"On the basis of different degrees of intellectual
capabilities such as the lower, the middle and
the higher, life itself can be divided into three
stages. The Scripture, out of compassion and
consideration, has taught this method of
worship or discipline for the benefit of those
who are not yet enlightened." (3.16)*

Interestingly enough, as outlined in Gaudapada's Karika above (3.16), Sankara also bifurcates the humanity into two categories comprising the enlightened and the ignorant respectively. The vast majority of people who belong to the second category (i.e. lacking enlightenment) cannot grasp non-duality, and Sankara posits that it is for their benefit that the scriptures contain passages pertaining to dualism.

Sankara tends to exhibit the impact of Gaudapada in another important area too, and this relates to use of similes. In Sankara's works one comes across again and again certain metaphors. His most well-known metaphor is that of rope-and-snake. Its implication is as follows. A man in darkness mistakes a rope for a snake and gets frightened. But his misapprehensions disappear as light dawns. In the same way with the onset of enlightenment the distorted picture of the reality which man perceives, thanks to his ignorance, is effaced, and is superseded by an altogether different vision of the Absolute. Gaudapada too in his works repeatedly alludes to the rope-and-snake metaphor to convey precisely the same message. Similarly, the simile of artificial division of space by pots and vessels is cited by both Sankara and Gaudapada. This is to bring out how in essence human soul cannot be differentiated from the Supreme Soul or Absolute. In the works of both these philosophers an impossible event is illustrated by comparing it to a barren woman giving birth to a son.

It is clear from what has preceded that Sankara indeed borrowed certain ideas and elements from Gaudapada's philosophy. But it needs to be emphasized that Sankara also differed from him in many crucial ways.

Gaudapada attached no importance to the worldly life. To him it was little more than a phantasmagoria. Sankara never decried the temporal life in this way. He called upon the common man to lead his life as per scriptural injunctions basing it on adherence to canons of ethics and righteousness. This is because, according to Sankara, it afforded an avenue, and, in fact, the only avenue, to the common man to cleanse himself of his passions, desires, etc., and thus qualify himself to attain supreme knowledge. Gaudapada's philosophy contains no words of advice for the common man – how he could uplift himself spiritually. On the other hand, concern over welfare of humanity formed a dominant facet of Sankara's life. Finally, Gaudapada hardly alluded to God in his writings; love for and faith in God were emotions alien to him. But to large segments of humanity worship of God has been a source of great solace and happiness. Sankara too had ardent faith in God; he regularly prayed in temples and his devotional poetry amply bears testimony to the profundity of his love for God.

It is clear from what has preceded that Gaudapada's

philosophy was indeed deficient in many key areas and differed from Advaitism in several crucial respects. This is why he can never be equated with Sankara. But there is no doubt that Gaudapada paved the way for formulation of Advaitism.

Quoting from a scholar:

[1]

> *"This discussion will also indicate how Gaudapada has practically prepared the entire ground for the great Samkaracarya. Samkaracarya had to move a step forward in clearing up some of the questions which Gaudapada did not care to discuss but for which he had either suggested, implied or indicated answer."*

We have been so far dealing with the first two queries posed at the beginning of this chapter, namely, the areas of similarity and dissimilarity between Advaitism and Gaudapada's philosophy. Let us now turn to the third query, i.e. assessing the impact on Gaudapada of idealist schools of Buddhism. There are three distinct areas in which one can clearly discern this influence.

First and foremost, it is the doctrine of Maya. The concept of Maya was earlier enunciated by the Mahayana school of Buddhism, and Gaudapada made it an integral part of his philosophy.

Many terms like 'Dharma', 'Dhata', 'Asparsayoga',

etc., found in Buddhist literature are liberally used by Gaudapada. More importantly, he borrows verbatim some of the verses composed by the famous Madhyamika philosopher Nagarjuna (who represented idealist schools), and makes them a part of his Karika.

Finally, Gaudapada too liberally makes use of the technique of dialectics earlier deployed by Buddhist philosophers with a view to clinching his arguments.

Here no doubt the following question will arise in the reader's mind: to what extent Sankara's approach was analogous to that of Gaudapada in these three above-mentioned arenas? This question is important because it helps one to appreciate how Sankara diverged from Gaudapada, while of course absorbing some elements from him.

As regards the doctrine of Maya, its formulation by Sankara was indeed vastly different from that by Gaudapada. To Sankara Maya was a divine entity; it was wonderful, beyond comprehension, ineffable. He repeatedly described Maya as an integral part of God. Such a depiction of Maya is totally absent in Gaudapada's works as well as in the texts authored by idealist schools of Buddhism. This is why, as brought out earlier, Sankara, unlike Gaudapada, attached profound importance to worldly life. As per Sankara, temporal life offered the common man the means, and the only means available at that, to improve himself spiritually. On the other hand, as per Gaudapada the worldly life was devoid of any import.

Sankara generally did not use the terms occurring in Buddhist literature, and when he did so, they usually carried a different meaning.   Unlike Gaudapada, Sankara did not include in his own writings verses of Nagarjuna or other Buddhist philosophers, barring one solitary exception.

Sankara no doubt deployed the technique of dialectics to buttress his arguments. But dialectics form a part of logic, and no special significance need be attached to this element of commonality between Sankara and Gaudapada.

It is thus evident that while Gaudapada borrowed elements from Buddhist ideology, these did not by and large form a part of Sankara's works. We have moreover already seen that Advaitism differs from Gaudapada's philosophy in many crucial respects. On the basis of the preceding, one can therefore definitely conclude that there was no justification for giving the appellation 'Crypto-Buddhist' to Sankara on account of the purported influence on him of Gaudapada as done by some of his critics.

Interestingly enough, both Gaudapada and Sankara were influenced by thoughts of early Buddhist savants who preceded the emergence of idealist schools of Buddhism. One reaches such a conclusion on the basis of an ancient Buddhist text whose translation in Chinese has survived the ravages of time. This text affirms that creation of the cosmos is an impossibility. This is because if the basic substratum of the universe is held to be eternal and immutable, it cannot give rise to anything which is marked by change as is our world.

This far-reaching and profound dogma is clearly enunciated in following two quotations adduced from this text:

> *"Because the presiding deity, the world-cause, is eternal, it will not be able to give rise to anything. This must be the same as in the case of space (Aksas) which can not produce anything, since it is eternal. Only something which is impermanent and perishable has the potential to give birth to another thing." (Tattva. VV 140, 147)*

> *"The effect must always have a homogeneity and resemblance with its cause. Therefore since the presiding deity is eternal, the phenomenal world, as its effect, must also be eternal. In effect, it can not be impermanent. But this assertion is contradicted by our experience of reality." (Tattva V, 138)*

It would be observed that both these quotations are implicitly postulating the dogma of identity of cause and effect. Gaudapada as mentioned earlier endorsed it and so did Sankara. (See Chapters IV and V.) Naturally, they too, like their ancient Buddhist forbears, reached the conclusion that in no way our world marked by diversity and flux could have emanated from undifferentiated, immutable Absolute.

It is thus seen how the genesis of Advaitism can be traced to the earliest speculation of Buddhist philosophers.

During the centuries preceding Sankara's times, Hindu metaphysics basically wrestled with the following fundamental metaphysical riddle:

God is omnipotent, omnipresent and eternally immutable. How could He then possibly create our world marked by imperfections and ephemerality?

This conundrum could be resolved in two ways.

God, thanks to His sublime power, could create this world without in any way losing His transcendent qualities like immutability, immanence, etc. This led to an influential school of philosophy called "Bheda-Abheda" which held much clout prior to Sankara's time. Unfortunately, nothing much is known about this school of philosophy or its proponents as all the ancient texts expounding it have been lost. But it may be mentioned in passing that this philosophy provides the metaphysical underpinning to Bhaktimarg.

Alternately it can be posited that no creation is possible. This naturally explains how God's sublime qualities are not sullied by the (apparent) emergence of our world. This postulate inevitably leads to Advaitism in which the temporal world is looked upon as less than real and its genesis is ascribed to Maya.

1: *The making of the Vedanta T. G. Mainkar, Published by Manshiram Manoharlal, Page 111.*

"Only through performance of action is there expatiation of sins accumulated through previous births. Hence no lay person should hope to make spiritual gains by forsaking action. Moreover, no benefit accrues from renunciation unaccompanied by supreme knowledge." [Sankara Bhashyam on Gita.]

"Discharge of obligatory duties is preferable to inaction. Moreover, continuation of life in a proper way is itself dependent on action." [Sankara Bhashyam on Gita.]

Chapter 8
Sankara: The Supreme Karmayogi

The very title of this chapter may evoke a degree of bewilderment in the reader. This is because it is believed by many, though erroneously, that Sankara solely advocated monasticism and called upon one and all to sever their links with the temporal world. There is indeed some justification for such a belief. Sankara's main texts like Vivekchoodamani, Atmabodha and Upadesa Sahasri exclusively focus on monasticism.

But Sankara himself never cut his ties with the world. He spent most of his life travelling in different parts of India, meeting people and counselling them as to the correct mode of leading their worldly lives. Spiritual upliftment of humanity always remained his paramount objective. He never advocated monasticism for the common man; in fact, he categorically affirmed that the common man was incapable of embracing Gyanamarg which presupposed the cognition of the transcendent Soul.

Sankara's espousal of Karmayoga comes out clearly in his Bhashyam on the Gita. This chapter therefore takes Sankara's Bhashyam on the Gita as the basis to show how he consistently exhorted the common man to observe Karmayoga.

Sankara right in the beginning of his Bhashyam on the

Gita affirms that the primary objective of Hinduism was to ensure material prosperity of humanity as well as to cater to its spiritual needs. He says:

1

> *"For, the dharma revealed in the Vedas is of two kinds - one characterized by action, and the other by renunciation. That dharma, which is meant for the stability of the world and is the direct means to both secular and spiritual welfare of living beings, continues to be followed by Brahmanas and others belonging to different castes and stages of lives, who aspire after the highest."*

> *"That dharma, characterized by action and enjoined for different castes and stages of life, even though it is meant for achieving prosperity and attaining heaven, yet, when performed with the attitude of dedication to God and without hankering for (selfish) result, leads to the purification of the internal organ. And, in the case of a person with a purified internal organ, it becomes the cause even of final liberation."*

The main tenets which Sankara enunciates in his Bhashyam on the Gita pertaining to Karmayoga can be succinctly put forth as follows:

1) Gyanamarg or Path of Knowledge represents the sole avenue leading to salvation.

2) Karmamarg leads to Gyanamarg through

purification of the Self.

3) Karmamarg is mandatory for all except the enlightened.

4) Righteousness must be upheld in worldly life.

These tenets form the leitmotiv of Sankara's Bhashyam on the Gita. This will become amply clear from what follows.

We start with Sankara's Bhashyam on Chapter ll of the Gita. As is well-known, this chapter lays down the basic parameters of Karmayoga in explicit terms. Sankara in his gloss on this chapter wholly concurs with its various hymns calling for observance of Karmayoga, and expresses no dissent whatsoever. This fact alone is therefore enough to establish that Sankara wholeheartedly endorsed Karmayoga and had no reservations about it.

Sankara advocates Karmayoga in order that virtue and morality may be upheld, and this is clearly seen from his gloss on hymn 2.31.

"The best course of action for a warrior is engagement in a righteous war."

Sankara also emphasizes again and again in his commentary on this chapter that it is absolutely essential for man to work with detachment and not to hanker after the possible benefits which may ensue from it. He is critical even of those who engage in rituals with a view to some gains, whether in this life or hereafter. Sankara's call to the common man to discharge his duties but to divorce them totally from their fruits is nothing but reaffirmation of the doctrine of Karmayoga. [SB. G. 2.42, 43, 44, 48]

Following doubt may assail the reader's mind here. Advaitism regards knowledge and action as mutually exclusive, as antithetical to each other. How did Sankara then espouse Karmayoga?

The answer to this query is very simple. Sankara never claimed that the same individual could simultaneously practise Karmayoga and Gyanayoga. Sankara contended that ordinary people were enjoined upon to adhere to Karmayoga while Gyanayoga was mandatory for the enlightened. He states this doctrine unambiguously and explicitly in his gloss on Chapter III.

Quoting from it.

> *"When humanity was created God proclaimed the way leading to prosperity and attainment of salvation. Those (Samkhyas) who possessed the cognition to differentiate between perishable and imperishable, between finite and transcendent, who had observed monasticism from youth and who thoroughly understood the Vedas were alone entitled to observe Gyanamarga while all other had to discharge their worldly duties as laid down in holy books as appropriate to their caste and stage of life (student, householder, etc.)."* [SB. G. 3.3]

This excerpt clearly brings out how Sankara divided humanity into distinct categories, ignorant and enlightened, and prescribed Karmamarg and Gyanamarg for them respectively. Sankara repeatedly averred that for all those who were not enlightened observance of Karmamarg was mandatory. He affirms this in most explicit terms possible as follows:

> 2
>
> *"Therefore, the gist of the topic under discussion is that action must be undertaken by one who is qualified (for action) but is unenlightened. In the verses beginning from ('A person does not attain freedom from action by abstaining from action' [3.4] and ending with, 'You perform the obligatory duties and, through inaction, even the maintenance of your body will not be possible' [3.8], it has been proved that before one attains fitness for steadfastness in the knowledge of the Self, it is the bounden duty of a person who is qualified for action, but is not enlightened, to undertake Karma-Yoga for that purpose. And then, also in the verses commencing from ['This man becomes bound by actions other than that action meant for God' [3.9] and ending with 'O Partha, he lives in vain,'] many reasons have been incidentally stated as to why a competent person has to undertake action; and the evils arising from their non-performance have also been emphatically declared.'*

But who was to be termed as enlightened? As per Sankara only the person who could differentiate the perishable body from the transcendent Soul could be so described (see the earlier quotation SB. G. 3.3). This obviously means that barring a microscopic minority everybody fell under the category of being 'not enlightened', and for this overwhelming majority Karmamarg was clearly prescribed by Sankara without any caveat whatsoever being attached.

In fact, Sankara goes to the extent of affirming that

even the enlightened sages were required to engage in worldly life for promotion of public weal. This would become evident from the following extract adduced from his Bhashyam on Chapter III.

> *"Warrior kings of the yore like Janaka, who were wise attained self-realization through action. Even assuming they were enlightened, they continued to perform their duties with a view to ensuring welfare of the society." [SB. G. 3.20]*

This is a highly significant pronouncement by Sankara because as per Advaitism, an enlightened sage transcends the realm of action. Such a sage therefore abjures all worldly activities including even those which are entirely altruistic in nature. That Sankara made Karmayoga applicable to even such a personage is reflective of the paramount importance which he attached to this doctrine.

Sankara fully agrees with the Gita in attaching overwhelming importance to promotion of public welfare. This would become evident from following quotation from his Bhashyam on Chapter III.

"Moreover, whether you (Arjuna) are enlightened like Me (Krishna Himself) or not, and even if you have no duty of your own, welfare of others should not be lost sight of." [SB. G. 3.25]

In his gloss on Verse 3.30, Sankara lays down how a common man should conduct himself. First he poses the query:

"How should a lay person (who is required to engage in Karmayoga), but who is also desirous of salvation, conduct himself?"

Sankara counsels as follows:

"Dedicate your actions to the omniscient Lord (Vasudeo) who exists in the hearts of all. Discharge your duties looking upon yourself as God's servant." [SB. G. 3.30]

This is nothing but advocacy of Karmayoga.

Thus Sankara reiterates again and again that Karmayoga was mandatory for an average individual and even extends its scope to enlightened sages even though this ran counter to a basic tenet of Advaitism. He gives utmost importance to welfare of the society and enjoins upon man to work towards its realization. One can therefore safely conclude that Sankara fully support s the doctrine of Karmayoga in toto as enunciated in Chapters II and III of the Gita. This is why one can say with every confidence that Sankara espoused the cause of Kamayoga without any reservations.

We have so far focused on Sankara's Bhashyam on Chapters II and III of the Gita as they are largely devoted to exposition of Karmayoga. Verses commending Karmayoga occur now and then in other chapters of the Gita too. Let us see how Sankara amplifies them.

Sankara's rationale behind advocacy of Karmoyoga can be clearly seen from the following text adduced from his gloss on Chapter IV of the Gita:

> *"If you (Arjuna) lack supreme knowledge, then you should follow Karmayoga to achieve self-purification; if you are already enlightened , then you should engage in action in the interest of public welfare." [SB. G. 4.15]*

It is noteworthy that an affirmation of this kind is not found in the Gita. Sankara clearly looked upon Karmamarg as the only avenue through which man could elevate himself spiritually. This would become clear from the following:

> *"Supreme Knowledge arises only from duly engaging in Karmayoga which cleanses one of accumulated sins. When man begins to doubt as to whether Karmayoga indeed leads to emancipation (by generating supreme knowledge in due course), he wreaks destruction on himself. (Therefore), Krishna urges Arjuna to discharge his duty to achieve self-realization. He thus*

appeals to him to rise up and go forth into the war." [SB. G. 4.42]

Sankara also explicitly lays down (something which the Gita does not do) that an ordinary person who lacked supreme knowledge was debarred from embracing Gyanayoga. This becomes evident from his gloss on verse 5.2 of the Gita:

"That the latter (Karmayoga) was preferable to the former (monasticism without discriminating Knowledge)." [SB. G. 5.2]

Since the vast majority of humanity was devoid of sublime knowledge, Sankara was clearly conveying that it was only the avenue of Karmayoga which was open before an average individual.

Similarly, in his amplification of certain verses in chapter 18 of the Gita advocating Karmayoga, Sankara extends their scope and puts additional emphasis on Karmayoga's observance. To give two instances: Verse 18.10 says "that a true Karmayogi is neither attached to agreeable actions, nor does he loath disagreeable ones". Sankara construes this verse more broadly as implying that a true Karmayogi should carry out all the activities, whether mundane or spiritual, in the same way. An extract from his gloss on this verse goes as:

"Agreeable action is one from which spiritual benefits accrue while disagreeable action connotes mundane tasks of daily life. Sankara counsels that a Karmayogi should perform all activities in the same way, without displaying

111

*any special preference for those which he deems
to be ennobling." [SB. G. 18.10]*

Similarly, Sankara's commentary on verse 18.56 is very significant. This verse says:

*"Despite being engaged in all actions, taking
refuge in Me, through My grace, one attains the
eternal, immutable abode."*

What does the phrase "all actions" signify in this hymn? Sankara clarifies as follows in his Bhashyam:

*"The term 'all actions' incorporates even those
acts which are normally prohibited."*

Sankara here is clearly more explicit than the original text in advocating greater involvement in worldly life.

We can therefore sum up the foregoing discussion by saying that Sankara indeed was a fervent champion of Karmayoga. Moreover, it also needs to be borne in mind that Sankara endorsed it on many occasions more strongly than the Gita itself. Such a conclusion proves inevitable in view of the following:

1. Sankara leaves no doubt that Karmayoga is mandatory for the entire humanity, whether one is an ordinary person or an enlightened being. Such an explicit affirmation in favour of Karmayoga is found wanting in the Gita. [SB. G. 4.15]

2. Sankara debars embracing of Gyanamarg by one who lacked supreme knowledge. There is again no such prescription in the Gita. [SB. G. 5.2]

3. Sankara considers Karmayoga as the only means through which an ordinary person can purge himself of his accumulated sins. The Gita never makes such a pronouncement categorically. [SB. G. 4.42]

A noteworthy feature of Sankara's Bhashyam on the Gita lies in its clear differentiation between ordinary people who are mired in ignorance and enlightened beings. The Gita, on the other hand, nowhere draws such a line of demarcation between ordinary people and enlightened beings, and this proves a source of confusion. The Gita, for instance, never specifies who should be engaged in daily life and who should renounce it.

Sankara removes many of the ambiguities in the Gita by construing some of its hymns as being applicable exclusively to those who had attained enlightenment. To give one instance: stanzas in chapter II from No. 55 onwards extol extreme dispassion and equanimity; they portray an ideal individual as somebody who has totally purged his mind of all hopes, desires, etc. But this can be a source of confusion. One cannot imagine how an ordinary householder engaged in daily existence can sever his links so completely with the life outside. Here Sankara clarifies that these verses were meant to apply only to those who had gained knowledge, and as such did not cover the ordinary people who were described as ignorant.

Sankara's criteria for portraying an individual as enlightened were extremely stringent. According to him, only that individual who had totally obliterated his consciousness as being a distinct entity and who saw himself as a part of the universe could be given this appellation. Even a great and noble warrior like Arjuna was deemed to be ignorant. It is thus evident that Sankara categorized for all practical purposes the entire humanity as "ignorant".

Sankara asks an ordinary individual to carry out all tasks of life, whether connected with mundane matters or spiritual, with the same spirit of dedication to God. He thus clearly implies that he expected an ordinary householder to take due interest in ensuring the welfare of himself and his family. Here again the Gita is somewhat ambiguous. It seems to convey that anybody who wishes to practise Karmayoga should be completely indifferent to his own interests. This is because it is only through extreme selflessness that man can relinquish his attachment to the fruits of his actions as enjoined upon by Karmayoga. But this calls for total eradication of one's ego which is tantamount to being enlightened.

Interestingly enough, Sankara gives far more leeway to the average individual and seems to accept that the vast majority of people cannot in one go dissociate themselves from their distinct, individual existence. He therefore explicitly states that the descriptions of a true Karmayogi as found in several verses of the Gita are applicable only to the sages and not to the average individual.

Sankara in this way envisions how an average individual can gradually become a better and better Karmayogi. He thus brings Karmayoga within the ken of the average person. This is again something which the Gita never does.

1:      *Gita   Bhashyam   by   Sankara.   Translated   by   Swami Gambhirananda.   Pages 3, 6 & &7.*

2:      *Ibid.   Pages 149 & 150.*

"Indeed nature, which is nothing but ignorance, acts and become affected. In this way empirical dealing becomes possible; but in reality it does not occur in the supreme Self." [Sankrara Bhashyam on Gita.]

"As the sun (reflected) in water is a part of the (actual) sun, and goes to the sun itself and does not return when the water, the cause of the reflection, is remove, so also even this part becomes similarly united wit that very Self; or, as space enclosed in a pot, etc., delimited by such adjuncts as the pot etc., being a part of space does not return after being united with space when the cause (of limitation), viz pot etc., is destroyed. This being so, it has been rightly stated, 'by reaching which they do not return'." [Sankara Bhashyam on Gita.]

This chapter focuses on bringing out how Advaitism finds ample endorsement in the Gita. It cogently establishes that many verses in the Gita will appear to be fatuous unless they are construed within the framework of Advaitism.

A lay reader will find it far from easy to accept the above proposition. This is because the doctrine of Maya which forms the linchpin of Advaitism finds no explicit mention in the Gita. What is more, even the word Maya occurs only three/four times in this scripture, and certainly does not carry the Advaitic connotation of illusionism. (See Chapter V.) Similarly, the Gita basically focuses on laying down how a man should lead his daily life, and represents a dialogue between God incarnate and man. All this again finds no parallel in any of Sankara's texts.

To bring out how Advaitism derives inspiration from Gita and to establish how the latter can only be understood within the framework of the former, we begin with Chapter 13 of the Gita. We have chosen this chapter because it mainly deals with metaphysics which also constitutes the core of Advaitism.

In this chapter, as elsewhere in the Gita, existence of a single transcendent entity which is immutable and immanent is predicated. But then what happens to our changing world?

Such a question inevitably arises as it is claimed that there exists nothing apart from the transcendent Absolute.

This Absolute called God, Soul, etc., is deemed to be the seer of the world. But since God is perfect, how does one account for imperfections of the world which is nothing but God's creation? How does one reconcile God's sublimity with the decadence of the world?

The Gita also ascribes the creation of the world to the union between perishable matter and the transcendent Absolute. But this appears to be an impossibility as what is finite cannot unite with what is infinite.

These are some of the basic conundrums which Gita poses in Chapter 13 and elsewhere; but it provides no answers to them.   Advaitism is able to resolve them elegantly by invoking the doctrine of Maya.   Let us see this in more detail.

We first turn to Stanza 13.2 which goes as:

> *"Know Me as the Knower-of-the-field in all fields, O Bharata; Knowledge of the field as also of the Knower-of-the-field is considered by Me to be (supreme) Knowledge."*

The word 'Me' connotes God here while the phrase 'Knower-of-the-field' signifies Soul. This stanza thus clearly enunciates the identity of Soul with God. The reader will recall that this represents a central dogma of Advaitism. (See Chapter IV.) But such a postulate immediately leads to following contradiction:

If God is no different from Soul, the existence of our temporal world will get negated. This is because there will be nothing left in the world except God. But such an assertion obviously conflicts with the reality as we perceive it. Sankara in his Bhashyam brings out this apparent dichotomy as follows:

1

> *"Objection: Well, if it be that in all the fields there exists God alone, and none else other than Him, as the enjoyer, then God will become a mundane being; or, due to the absence of any mundane creature other than God, there will arise the contingency of the negation of mundane existence. And both these are undesirable, since the scriptures dealing with bondage, liberation and their causes will become useless and also because they contradict such valid means of Knowledge as direct perception."*
> *[SB. G. 13.2]*

Sankara resolves this dilemma by invoking the doctrine of Maya. As per Advaitism, our world of plurality gets superimposed on the Absolute due to ignorance and hence the former is not affected by the latter. It may be recalled from Chapter V that the world is looked upon as a creation of Maya and the only reality in the ultimate sense is deemed to be that of Brahman. Sankara gives the metaphor of sky and dust, pointing out that dust in no way disfigures the sky though the two are in contact. In this metaphor dust stands for the world while the sky symbolizes the Absolute. Sankara then argues that in the same way though God inhabits the human body, He remains untarnished, untainted.   Quoting in Sankara's words:

2

"This being so, the mundane state, consisting of agentship and enjoyship pertaining to the objects of Knowledge is superimposed on the Knower through ignorance.   Hence, nothing of the knower is affected thereby-in the same way as nothing of the sky is affected by the superimposition of surface, dirt, etc. (on it) by fools. Such being the case, not the least touch of the mundane state is to be apprehended with regard to the almighty God, t he Knower of the field, even though He exists in all the fields. For it is nowhere seen in the world that anybody is benefited or harmed by a quality attributed to him through ignorance." [SB. G. 13.2]

Turning now to two next verses of the Gita:

"I shall speak of that which is to be known, by realizing which one attains Immortality. The Supreme is without any beginning. That is called neither being nor non-being." [13.12]

"That (Knowable) which has hands and feet everywhere, which has eyes, heads and mouths everywhere, which has ears everywhere, exists in creatures by pervading them all." [13.13]

These two verses appear to be mutually contradictory. This is because the first verse portrays Brahman as transcendent since it is deemed to be both being and non-being. But the second verse ascribes anthropomorphic features to It which obviously negate Its transcendence.   How does one shed light on this dichotomy?

Sankara resolves this enigma by affirming that the so-called hands, feet, etc., of Brahman are nothing but a manifestation of Maya, and hence are not entirely real. They therefore in no way conflict with Brahman's transcendence. He says that such human features belong to Brahman only in a figurative sense as they as they owe their existence to Its power.

Quoting in Sankara's words:

3

> "*All diversity in the Knower of the field, caused by the differences in the adjunct-the field-is certainly unreal.*"

> "*Everywhere the hands, feet, etc., which are perceived as limbs of all bodies perform their duties due to the presence of the power of the Knowable (Brahman). Thus the grounds for the inference of the existence of the Knowable are metaphorically spoken of as belonging to the Knowable.*" [SB. G. 13.12, 13.13]

Turning to another verse of Chapter 13, which appears to pose a riddle:

> "*And undivided, yet He exists as if divided in beings; That is to be Known as the supporter of beings; He devours and He generates.*" [13.16]

Sankara's gloss on this verse is highly illuminating. He takes recourse to his favourite metaphor of artificial division of space by pots, vessels, etc., which finds repeated mention in his various works. Sankara turns to this metaphor to illustrate how Brahman while One in truth appears as if apportioned into multitudes of human beings thanks to the illusive role of Maya. It is thus implied that the so-called division of Brahman into human bodies is as illusory as the figurative partitioning of space by pots, vessels, etc.

But how does one make sense of so-called creative and destructive roles of Brahman as ascribed to It in the second line of stanza 13.16? This seems an impossibility as Brahman is immutable and totally devoid of activity. Sankara easily gets around this hurdle. He puts forth his favourite simile of snake and rope. He says that just as due to darkness, the rope is mistaken for the snake, in the same way thanks to Maya the undifferentiated Brahman is looked upon as the multi-faceted world. The appearance of the world therefore like that of the snake is not wholly real.   Similarly, the destruction of the world like the purported disappearance of the snake lacks reality.   Thus, it is only an imagery when creation and destruction are attributed to Brahman since in the ultimate sense both don't occur. [SB.G. 13.16]

Turning to another verse from the Gita:

> *"Whatever object, moving or non-moving, comes into being, Know that to be from the association of the field and the Knower-of-the-field." [SB. G. 13.26]*

This verse speaks of something which is seemingly

impossible, namely, the union between perishable matter (field) and imperishable soul (knower-of-the-field). Sankara contends that such a contradiction arises due to our improper understanding. In reality there is no tangible interaction between the transcendent and the ephemeral. While in Reality the latter is merely superimposed on the former, man in his ignorance construes it as the union between the two. The formulation of this riddle and its resolution are best given in Sankara's inimitable style:

4

> *"Objection: what, again, is meant by this association of the field and the Knower-of-the-field? Since the-Knower-of-the-field is partless like space, therefore its conjunction with the field cannot be a kind of relationship like coming together of a rope and a pot through the contact of their parts. Nor can it be an intimate and inseparable relation as between a thread and a cloth, since it is not admitted that the field and the Knower of the field are mutually related by way of being cause and effect."* [SB. G. 13.26]

This is answered as:

5

> *"The association of the field and the Knower-of-the-field which are the object and the subject, respectively, and are of different natures – is in the form of superimposition of each on the other as also of their qualities, as a consequence of the absence of discrimination between the real natures of the field and the Knower-of-the-field.*

*This is like the association of a rope, nacre, etc.,
with the superimposed snake, silver etc., owing
to the absence of discrimination between them.
This association of the field and the Knower-of –
the-field in the form of superimposition is
described as false Knowledge."* [SB. G. 13.26]

Another bewildering verse in chapter 13 to which
Sankara proffers an elegant explanation within the framework
of Advaitism is the following:

*"Indeed, he who sees the same Lord everywhere
equally dwelling, destroys not the Self by the
Self; therefore, he goes to the Highest Goal."*
[13.28]

Here Sankara raises a highly pertinent query. How
could Self be destroyed since it is well known to be immutable?

Sankara's explanations runs as follows:

*An ordinary man fails to differentiate
imperishable Soul from the perishable body. He
thus figuratively anniilates It through his
ignorance. But a wise man does not commit
such an error, and thus knowing Reality attains
communion with God. [SB. G. 13.28]*

Finally, we will cite two verses from chapter 13 which
cannot be construed outside the Advaitic framework. In fact,

they appear to propound the basic doctrines of Advaitism, though in an oblique and implicit way. These verses are:

> *"When one realizes that the state of diversity of living things is rooted in the one, and that their manifestation is also from that, then one becomes identified with Brahman."* [13.30]

> *"Being without beginning and without qualities, this immutable, supreme Self does not act, nor is It affected, although existing in the body."* [13.31]

The first verse obviously affirms the basic Advaitic dogma regarding immanence of Brahman and there being nothing devoid of It. When one realizes this fact, the stanza says, one attains union with Brahman. But this is precisely the state of salvation or enlightenment as visualized in Advaitism. (See Chapter IV.) As per its basic tenet, man becomes Brahman when he cognizes that the world lacks reality and there is nothing in the ultimate sense apart from Brahman.

As regards the second hymn,, it raises the following age-old paradox: how to account for God's (or Soul's) involvement in the world without there being any impairment of His sublimity or transcendence?

Sankara poses this dilemma in following terms:

6

> *" Who is it, again, that acts in the body and becomes affected? On the one hand, if there be some embodied being other than the Self who*

127

*acts and becomes affected, then sayings such as,
'And also understand Me to be Knower-of-the-
field', that the Knower-of-the-field and God are
one, would lose their validity. Again, if there be
no embodied being who is different from God,
then it has to be stated who is it that acts and
gets affected. Or it has to be asserted that the
supreme one does not exist. Thus, since the
Upanishadic philosophy as stated by the Lord is
in every way difficult to understand and difficult
to explain, it has therefore been abandoned by
the Vaisesikas, the Sankhyas, the Jainas and the
Buddhists." [SB.G. 31]*

Invoking the doctrine of Maya, Sankara elucidates the above conundrum as follows:

7

*"Indeed, Nature, which is nothing but
ignorance, acts and becomes affected. In this
way empirical dealing become possible; but in
reality it does not occur in the Supreme Self."*
[SB.G. 31]

Sankara basically contends that the world being a manifestation of Maya can in no way detract from the pristine sublimity of God.

Chapter 13 is perhaps the most important part of the Gita in terms of its metaphysical content. We saw in earlier paragraphs how its verses can be elegantly construed within the framework of Advaitism, and especially on the basis of the doctrine of Maya. We also saw how some of them even appear to enunciate fundamental Advaitic dogmas, though not explicitly. This is why we said at the beginning of this chapter that Advaitsim is very much in consonance with the underlying philosophy of Gita.

Let it, however, not be thought that it is only the verses of chapter 13 which substantiate Advaitism. In fact, one needs to rely on Advaitism, especially its doctrine of Maya, to properly understand many of the verses in other chapters of the Gita too. This will become clear from the following:

Turning to chapter II:

> *"He who knows this one as indestructible, eternal, birthless and undecaying how and whom does that person kill or whom does he cause to be killed."* [2.21]

This hymn prima facie appears to be nothing more than fatuous. It seems to imply that an enlightened being is incapable of killing anybody. Sankara says in his gloss that the word "Kill" needs to be construed in a figurative sense as signifying any kind of action. But such an interpretation seems to make this hymn even more perplexing as it would mean that a wise man is incapable of undertaking any activity. This sounds preposterous.

Sankara here recalls the cardinal Advaitic doctrine that in a state of enlightenment the wise man realizes that the world around him is nothing but a play of Maya. In such a state he feels that he is as immutable as the Supreme Self and therefore comes to look upon all actions attributed to him as nothing but an illusion.

This is how Sankara elucidates this hymn. Quoting from his gloss on it:

8

"Because the man of Knowledge is one with the Self. Enlightenment does not belong to the aggregate of body and senses. Therefore, as the last alternative, the knower is the Immutable and is the Self which is not a part of the aggregate. Thus, action being impossible for that man of Knowledge." [SB. G. 2.21]

1:   Sankara Bhashya on the Gita translated by Swami Gambhirananda. Advaita Ashram. 5, Delhi. Calcutta. Page 497
2:   Ibid. Page 501
3:   Ibid. Pages 531 & 532
4:   Ibid. Page 555
5:   Ibid. Pages 555 & 556
6:   Ibid. Page 563
7:   Ibid. Page 564
8:   Ibid. Page 64

"To the Self who, deluded by Maya sees, in dreaming and waking, the universe in its distinctions, such as cause and effect, property and proprietor, disciple and teacher, and father and son, likewise to Him, of the form of the Preceptor, the blessed Daksinamurti may this obeisance be." [Hymns to Daksinamurti.]

"Those who have the firm knowledge that the Supreme Reality is such alone and not otherwise are called drdhavratah (steadfast in their resolve) and (they) adore Me, the Supreme Self." [Sankara Bhashyam on Gita.]

Chapter 10

God of Sankara:
Personal or Impersonal

This chapter aims to analyse the perspective of Advaitism towards Bhaktimarg and Personal God. Advaitism has been widely misunderstood on this score. It is held by many that Sankara relegated Bhaktimarg to a secondary place vis-a-vis Gyanamarg. It is also claimed by such circles that medieval saints like Ramanuja and Madhava subsequently reinstated Baktimarg in its rightful position and that they in turn denigrated Gyanamarg. This chapter examines these and related themes so as to project before the reader the correct message of Advaitism and Sankara.

We saw in an earlier chapter how Sankara perceived no dichotomy between monism and theism, and how, while propounding the doctrine of attributeless Brahman, his heart was suffused with piety and faith. He blessed construction of temples and used to regularly pray before idols. His devotional poetry overflows with love of God (see Chapter 6). We are going to look in more depth into this aspect of Sankara's personality and teachings in what follows. In particular, we will focus upon:

i) How Sankara envisaged the relationship between three paths to salvation, Karmamarg, Bhaktimarg and Gyanamarg. As we shall see, Sankara looked upon Bhaktimarg and

Gyanamarg as running in parallel directions. To him Bhakti and Gyana, which act as conduits to God and Brahman, were two sides of the same coin.

ii) Visualization of the Absolute in scriptures, both as Personal God as well as Impersonal Brahman.

iii) How Sankara identifies Personal God with Impersonal Brahman.

iv) How in Sankara's writings one finds insistence on both possession of sublime knowledge (Gyana) as well as reposing complete faith in God.

v) Analysis of the possible factors which have led some scholars to conclude that Hinduism perceives a conflict between Gyana and Bhakti or considers the two visualizations of godhead, Brahman and God, as mutually exclusive.

This chapter is almost entirely based on Sankara's Bhashyam on the Gita. It may be wondered why Sankara's other major texts like Sankara Bhashyam and Vivekchoodamani have not been consulted. This is because these texts deal with a number of complex metaphysical issues which are not germane to this chapter. In the Gita the Absolute is depicted as both God and Brahman. Therefore, Sankara's Bhashyam on it gives us a penetrating analysis as to the relationship conceived by Sankara between these two manifestations of godhead as well as how he drew no sharp line of differentiation between the means of attaining them i.e. Bhakti and Gyana, or devotion and knowledge. On the other hand, in Sankara's other texts this theme has not received special attention. In what follows the word Bhashyam will connote Sankara's Bhashyam on the Gita unless otherwise specified.

We will start with a review of the close symbiotic linkage as envisaged by Sankara between Bhaktimarg, Gyanamarg and Karmamarg.

Sankara always claimed that Karmamarg and Bhaktimarg were closely intertwined with each other. One sees this clearly from his commentary on various verses in the Gita which prescribe Karmamarg. While upholding Karmamarg, Sankara insists that a spiritual aspirant should keep his mind focused on God. He held that it was impossible for man to be a Karmayogi if he was not also a Bhaktiyogi at the same time. For instance, while amplifying verse 5-10 of Gita, Sankara says in his Bhashyam that "man should have a firm conviction that he was working for God as a servant does for his master".

It has been earlier brought out (see Chapter VIII) that Sankara held Karmamarg to be mandatory for all human beings except those who had attained enlightenment. Since he regarded Karmamarg and Bhaktimarg to be inalienable, it is clear that in his view the vast majority of mankind was expected to simultaneously observe both Karmamarg and Bhaktimarg. This is how he exhorted an ordinary individual to uplift himself spiritually and to become qualified to observe Gyanamarg.

Turning now to the relationship as perceived by Sankara between Bhaktimarg and Gyanamarg: there are a number of verses in the Gita which only extol Bhaktimarg and do not mention Gyanamarg at all. It is noteworthy that Sankara fully endorses them and in no way adds any caveat to the effect that Bhakti needs to be complemented by Gyana. This evidently implies that Sankara did not differentiate between Gyana and Bhakti.

Quoting from his Bhashyam:

1

> *"However, prostration, etc., which are external, are not invariably fruitful, for there is scope for dissimulation, etc. But this is not in the case of one possessing faith etc., Hence they are the unfailing means of acquiring knowledge." [SB. G. 4.39]*

Here Bhakti is portrayed as a pathway to Gyana. In fact, Sankara regarded knowledge and faith as two sides of the same coin. He says at one place in his Bhashyam:

2

> *"Bhakti through devotion, through that devotion described as knowledge." [SB. G. 18.55]*

He envisaged such an intimate link between Bhakti and Gyana that he could not contemplate the former without the latter. This would become amply evident from the following quotation taken from his Bhashyam:

3

> *"(This Supreme Person) is reached through ananyaya, one-pointed bhaktya, through devotion, characterized as knowledge; ananyaya,*

which is one pointed, which relates to the Self."
[SB. G. 8.22]

At the ultimate stage of salvation Sankara did not at all distinguish between Gyana and Bhakti, looking upon the latter as a necessary concomitant of the former. This is amply borne out by his portrayal of an enlightened being:

4

> *"On the contrary, those who have realized non-duality do not make any effort to arrange for themselves the acquisition of what they do not have, the preservation of what they have. Indeed, they desire nothing for themselves, in life or in death. They have taken refuge only in the Lord . Therefore the Lord Himself arranges to procure what they do not have and protect what they have got." [SB. G. 9.22]*

This quotation brings out how according to Sankara an enlightened being possessing supreme knowledge, who has experienced the unity of the cosmos, always surrenders himself totally to God and looks upon Him as the sole refuge. This is how Sankara envisaged merger of monism with theism.

We are now in a position to sum up Sankara's perspective towards various avenues to salvation. No doubt, as repeatedly affirmed by him in Vivekchoodamani (see Chapter IV), he considered Gyanamarg as the only path leading to salvation. But he knew that Gyanamarg could be embraced only by that rare individual who could adhere to harsh monasticism and who could differentiate body from soul. He advocated Karmamarg and Bhaktimarg for the vast majority of mankind and looked upon them as pathways to Gyanamarg. Moreover, he identified Bhakti with Gyana at the ultimate stage. He thus in no way consigned Bhaktimarg to a secondary status vis-a-vis Gyanamarg as claimed by some of his critics.

It would be pertinent to quote here from a scholar, Dr. Krishna:

[5]

> *"For example, Bhakti is interpreted as the theistic alternative to the "intellectualism" of the Advaita Vedanta of Sankaracharya. The contention is, that since the latter emphasises the importance of jnana, it leaves no room for Bhakti. Such assumptions are made by interpreting jnana as mere intellectual knowledge of god. But Sankara never used the term jnana in that sense. He invariably used it for the knowledge derived from personal spiritual experience and "Self-realisation". The difference between Jnana and mere intellectual understanding of it is stated clearly by him while recognizing the superiority of the former. The view that Bhakti is incompatible with the Advaita Vedanta is also a fallacy."*

Let us now see how Sankara in his works identifies Brahman and God with each other. However, before we do so, it would be pertinent to analyse how the scriptures deal with these two visualizations of the Absolute.

We start with the Vedas. As is well known, these texts abound with descriptions of anthropomorphic deities. They are very much Personal gods. But it will be wrong to presume that the concept of Impersonal Absolute was unknown to the ancient Vedic seers.

One of the oldest hymns in the Vedas is the "Nasidiya Sukta".   Its central theme relates to the impossibility of delineating the primordial substance or entity that existed at the time of genesis of the cosmos.   The author of this hymn makes it clear that what existed before the universe came into being was indeed something which defied human imagination and which could not be expressed within the parameters known to man.   This primordial entity (alluded to by terms like "It" and "Unit") has been portrayed in this hymn in self-contradictory terms such as 'neither what is', 'nor what is not.' Nasidiya Sukta therefore unmistakably shows that the ancient Vedic seers had clearly grasped the concept of 'Impersonal God'.

Turning now to the Upanisads: here the overwhelming focus is on Brahman, which is nothing but Impersonal God. Brahman is portrayed in differing ways in these texts and occasionally the genesis of the world is ascribed to It.   But by and large it is the ineffable, incomprehensible nature of Brahman divorced from the temporal world that is highlighted by them.   Thus the Upanisads mainly focus on depicting attributeless Brahman.   However, we do come across passages in these texts which speak about God endowed with human qualities.   So here too the godhead is described both in impersonal as well as personal terms.

Turning now to the third major scripture of Hinduism, the Gita. In this work again the picture is no different.   The Gita is largely a theistic text since it revolves around Lord Krishna. Lord Krishna was a man as well as a god.   No better example of Personal God can be adduced than that of Lord

Krishna. But even in a text like Gita, one comes across numerous references to Brahman, the Impersonal Absolute.

It is thus seen that in the scriptures both the visualizations of godhead run side by side. One comes across this feature also in various sacred texts which were composed subsequently.

Turning now to Sankara, he too followed the above pattern. In some of his major works like Atmabodha and Vivekchudamani his overwhelming emphasis has been on the Impersonal Absolute. But, as seen earlier, Sankara was also a great devotee with fervent faith in God; in his devotional poems, he goes to great lengths in ascribing gross corporeal features such as beauty and charm to various deities (see Chapter VI). Thus, though Sankara was primarily a monist, he was indubitably an ardent theist too. This is why in his writings Sankara portrayed the Absolute as both Impersonal Brahman as well as Personal God.

But the reader should not think that Sankara merely followed the precedent laid down by the scriptures and broke no new ground. What is noteworthy is that he was the first savant who clearly identified the Personal God with the Impersonal One. Let us see how he did so.

Sankara in his works often delineated the Absolute, both in personal terms as well as impersonal, in the same verse, in the same passage, thus leaving no room for doubt that in his view they were one and the same. Given below are quotations from his various texts which illustrate how he did so.

Sankara composed eleven hymns dedicated to

Sri Dakshinamurti, as Personal God, as Supreme Guru. This is why each of these hymn ends on the refrain: "to Him of the form of the preceptor, the blessed Dakshinamurti, may this obeisance be". But these hymns also describe the Guru as non-dual Self as would become clear from the examples cited below:

6

"To Him who by Maya as by dream, sees within Himself the universe which is inside Him, like unto a city that is seen in a mirror, (but) which is manifested as if without: to Him who apprehends, at the time of awakening, His own non-dual Self: to Him, of the form of the Preceptor, the blessed Daksinamurti may this obeisance be."

7

"To the Self who, deluded by Maya sees, in dreaming and waking, the universe in its distinctions, such as cause and effect, property and proprietor, disciple and teacher, and father and son, likewise-to him, of the preceptor, the blessed Daksinamurti may this obeisance be."

These hymns clearly sow how in Sankara's writings the distinction between Personal and Impersonal God tends to be obliterated.

Following passage will bring this out further:

8

"In my heart do I worship Siva who is knowable through the three Vedas, who is delightful to the

Here Siva is invested with gross human features. He is thus very much a Personal God. But he is also depicted as 'basic consciousness' which is an attribute of Impersonal God. Thus, in this hymn the personal and impersonal aspects of godhead merge together.

In Sankara's Bhashyam on the Gita one comes across several instances where the personal and impersonal attributes of the Absolute blend into each other. To give one such instance: the verse 7.19 of the Gita goes as: "At the end of several lives, the man of knowledge surrenders unto Me, knowing that Vasudeo alone is all this ...."

This hymn glorifies Vasudeo - Krishna as the paramount Personal God. But Sankara in his Bhashyam depicts Him in starkly impersonal phraseology as follows: "Me, Vasudeo, who is the inmost thing ..... Vasudeo is all; such a one who realizes Me thus as the Self of all (SB. G. 7.19)

To give another instance: The Gita describes God in vividly anthropomorphic terms as follows:

all wonders, effulgent, boundless, with innumerable faces on all sides. (Gita 11.11)

Notwithstanding the description of God in such gross terms, Sankara in his Bhashyam on this hymn brings in the impersonal aspect of godhead by saying interalia:

"He being the Self of all beings." (SB. G. 11. 11)

We thus see how in Sankara's writings the descriptions of godhead in personal and impersonal terms merge into each other. This aspect of Sankara's works is far from properly appreciated.

One might wonder here how Sankara could identify Personal God with Impersonal when they possessed conflicting attributes. To Sankara such an identification posed no dilemma. This is for the following simple reason. We hold that the Impersonal God and Personal God are endowed with features which are mutually exclusive because we think within the framework and constraints of our senses and perceptions; but God by definition totally transcends our phenomenal world, and, therefore, what may appear to be absolutely irreconcilable to us will have no such implication at the level of the Absolute.

Since Sankara thus did not differentiate between the personal and impersonal manifestations of God, he also did not draw a line of demarcation between Bhakti and Gyana. We had seen earlier how Sankara uses these terms interchangeably when it comes to portrayal of an enlightened being. One also sees this clearly in his collection of poems 'Bhaj Govindam' in which he pays homage to Lord Krishna. While these are devotional poems, they very much call upon the devotee to cognize the oneness of the cosmos as well as appreciate the fact that our changing temporal world does not represent the true Reality.

This would become evident from following verses taken from the above work:

9

"Who are you? Who am I? Whence have I come? Who is my mother? Who, my father? Thus enquire, leaving aside the entire world which is comparable to a dream, and is essenceless."

Here the world is described as devoid of reality, thus implying that the only Reality is that of immutable Brahman. The devotee is called upon to acquire this supreme knowledge or Gyana.

To give another instance:

10

"In you, in me, and elsewhere too, there is but one Visnu (God). Vainly do you get angry with me, being impatient. See the Self in all things, and leave off everywhere ignorance which is the cause of difference."

This hymn which is theistic in orientation speaks abut essential unity of the cosmos.

We thus see that in the spiritual symphony composed by Sankara, Bhakti and Gyana were clearly the two most dominant notes. Strangely enough, he is accused of having deprecated Bhakti and of propagating the view that salvation could be attained only through Gyana.

It is also held in some circles that medieval saints like Ramanuja and Madhava exclusively preached the gospel of faith, and rejected Advaitism because it gave primacy to Gyana. However, when one peruses the works of Ramanuja, Madhava and other medieval saints, one finds that the above argument is not strictly valid. No doubt, these saints castigated Sankara's doctrine of Maya and to this extent they certainly renudiated Advaitism (see Chapter V), but they never claimed that Sankara rejected Bhakti or that he was opposed to worship of personal God. On the other hand, these medieval saintsxqlwo did not in any way belittle the role of Gyana in achieving communion with the Absolute. In fact, like Sankara, they too looked upon Gyana and Bhakti as inalienably linked to each other. This was readily acknowledged in earlier centuries.

This is why we find that a 16th century text called Bhaktimala had lumped together Sankara with savants like Ramanuja and Madhava and described them all as proponents of Bhaktimarg. Quoting from Dr. Sharma:

11

> *"The Bhakta Mala includes a variety of religious personalities holding different viewpoints. The Advaita Vedantin Sankara, the Vaishnava acharyas, Madhava, Nimbarka etc., (whose difference with Sankara are too well known), are all treated as bhaktas. There is no indication in*

We see from what has preceded that the two manifestations of the Absolute, personal and impersonal, were not treated as distinct in the ancient scriptures. Subsequently, Sankara carried forward this process, and virtually identified them with each other. Moreover, he looked upon Bhakti and Gyana, which are conduits to Personal and Impersonal God, as two sides of the same coin.

In the writings of medieval saints known for their devotional fervour, one comes across no attempt to downgrade Gyana. One therefore wonders how the view gained ground that there was some conflict between Gyana and Bhakti, and that Sankara was indifferent to the latter.

The genesis of this misconception can be traced to the works of early Christian theologians and their writings on Hinduism. They were much influenced by the outlook of contemporary European philosophers. In Europe a clear trend towards differentiating philosophy from religion began to emerge from 16th century or so. Knowledge got linked with philosophy, while faith was deemed to be an essential concomitant of religion. This is how faith and knowledge came to be distinguished from each other. The European writers analysed Hindu texts through the prism of such opinions and perceptions. Naturally, their interpretation of them was one-sided and biased. Let us see how all this came about.

Philosophy as a separate discipline began to emerge in Europe after the reformation when philosophers started to conjecture as to the nature of the Absolute, the genesis of the cosmos, and other metaphysical issues without being fettered by the dogmas of Christianity.   This was itself an event of major significance in the evolution of metaphysical thought in Europe at that juncture.

It was believed in Europe until then that whatever was contained in Bible was the absolute truth, and that it furnished man with the totality of knowledge which he needed to have about the origin of the world, about life after, about divinity, and so on.   Thus, the search of European philosophers for truth outside the framework of Christianity led from the beginning to a cleavage between philosophy and religion.   Incidentally, this is something which never happened in case of Hinduism.   To give an instance of how European philosophers three/four centuries ago dissociated themselves from religion: following lines were inscribed on the tomb of a Spanish philosopher named Pascal:

12

"God of Abraham, God of Issac, God of Jacob not of philosophers and savants."

The Absolute envisaged by these philosophers was marked by perfection, by infinitude and so on, but certainly the attributes of love, forgiveness, etc., of the God of Christianity were not ascribed to It.   Subsequently, philosophers like Hegel came to pose a direct challenge to Christianity when they averred that the Absolute of philosophy was no different from the God of Christianity, arguing that there could not be two truths about the Absolute. Hegel built a system of philosophy which, while recognizing God, had no place for revelations, Gospels of Christ, etc.; his God was divorced from love and mercy.   Similarly, Hegel did not postulate that God could be reached only through devotion and faith.   Hegel's conception of the Absolute bore tantalizing resemblance to what Sankara had put forth a millennium ago.   Quoting from him:

13

> "The object of religious attitude is the absolute in its unity, in it completeness and in it truth."

It is clear from above that there was no place for faith in the scheme of the universe as envisaged by Hegel.   This was the viewpoint of other philosophers too.   On the other hand, to Christian theologians faith was the very essence of their religion.   Christianity's perspective in this regard has been put forth by a scholar as follows:

14

> "Similarly, only faith and feelings could be accepted as the true ingredients of religion. Intellectual inquiries and reasoning about the nature of God, and all explanations of Him in impersonal and abstract terms, amounted to nothing more than philosophical speculations. The Christian academic exercise to explain God strictly as a personality-and religion, as a realm different from that of philosophy – was almost complete by the middle of the nineteenth century."

This is how by the time the 19th century ended, philosophers and theologians came to occupy diametrically opposite positions.

The early Indologists who began to study Hinduism were mostly practising Christians. To them it was a self-evident axiom that religion needed to be based on a Personal God who was endowed with the attributes of love, mercy, etc.

They were impressed by Vaishnava literature as it glorifies Personal God and lays much emphasis on devotion and rituals. In the same way the Gita appealed to those scholars which they construed as a wholly theistic text devoted to exaltation of Krishna, the archetypal Personal God.

These Indologists then concluded that proper or true Hinduism was propounded only by the Gita and other Vaishnava texts whose main message, as per their interpretation, was exaltation of Personal God, and His visualization as a pre-eminent Being Who bestowed mercy and grace on man and enjoined him to engage in His worship. On the other hand, these scholars dismissed the Upanisadic texts as an example of dry intellectualism and categorized them as philosophy. They characterized them as primarily dealing with Impersonal God.

In this way Hinduism came to be looked upon as setting forth two distinct doctrines: one of Personal God and another of Impersonal God. Thus Bhakti and Gyana began to be looked upon as divorced from each other, and Hindu texts similarly got compartmentalized-some were said to be exclusively devoted to Personal God while others were deemed to be focused on Impersonal God.

Quoting here from Dr. Sharma:

15

"Drawing a distinction between religion and philosophy, they (the Indologists) used the two

as separate yard-sticks and classed the bulk of the religio-philosophical thought of the Hindus as "Brahminism", and their sectarian religious tradition and beliefs as " Hinduism". They placed Vaishnavism under the latter category, thus separating it from the Brahmanic tradition. Describing the religion of the Vedas as a mere expression of the "reverential awe of the forces of Nature and a desire to propitiate them", and Brahminism, as "simply an Indian variety of pantheism", they evolved the theory that in the general mass of Hinduism, the evidence of true montheism and "the essential elements of genuine religion" could be found only in Vaishnavism. These judgements were obviously based on their orthodox and formalised Christian concepts of god, religion, and monotheism. No description of God-other than personal-could satisfy them."

In a milieu like this is it any surprise that Sankara was depicted as an opponent of theism? B.G. Bhandarkar, perhaps the first Indian Indologist, was to say:

16

"Sankara's Advaitism is destructive of Bhakti as prescribed by Vaishnavism."

In this way, the seamless web of Hinduism was artificially segmented and its different segments were associated with one theme or another to the exclusion of all other. This is how through ignorance the basic purport of Hindu texts was totally misconstrued. Thus, Personal God and

Impersonal God, Bhakti and Gyana, came to be looked upon as diametrically different from, if not antithetical to, each other. In the process it was conveniently forgotten that to Sankara monism and theism constituted twin planks of the single edifice of Hinduism.

1:    Sankara Bhashyam on the Gita translated by Swami Gambhirananda. Advaita Ashram. 5 Delhi. Calcutta. Page 228.
2:    Ibid. Page 729
3:    Ibid. Page 360. Bracket by the author
4:    Ibid. Page 389
5:    Bhakti and Bhakti movement - A New Perspective. By Krishna Sharma. Published by Manoharlal Pvt. Ltd. Page. 43
6:    Sivanandalohari.   From hymns of Sankara.   By T.P.M. Mahadevan. Munshiram Manoharlal. Page 2
7:    Ibid. Page 21
8:    Ibid. Page 86
9:    Ibid. Page 68
10:   Ibid. Page 69
11:   S.No. 5. Ibid. Pages 71 & 72
12:   Ibid. Page 95
13:   Ibid. Page 103
14:   Ibid. Pages 106, 107 & 108
15:   Ibid. Page 78
16:   Ibid. Page 90

"The saints call it the Root. It is neither big nor little, neither long nor short, neither burning like fire nor flowing like water, without shadow, without darkness, without wind, without air, without attachment, without touch, taste, sight, smell, without hearing, speaking, thinking; without breath, without face, without energy, without measure, without inside or outside; it consumes nothing, nothing consumes it."

[From Brahad - Aranyaka Upanisad.]

Chapter 11

From Upanisads to Advaitism: Continuum or Transition

One comes across repeated references in Sankara's works to the effect that whatever was being· affirmed or concluded was in conformity with the Sruti and Smriti. By Sruti he obviously meant Upanisads. Sankara deemed these texts as an infallible source of knowledge and any argument or inference which contradicted them was ipso facto held by him to be invalid.

Though there are one hundred and ten (110) Upanisads, only eleven (11) of them are regarded as important. Sankara wrote commentaries on all of them, and showed how their various verses could be elegantly construed and understood within the framework of Advaitism. It would become clear from what follows that many verses in the Upanisads would seem to be paradoxical or fatuous unless one unravels them with the help of the doctrine of Maya.

In following paragraphs we have reviewed Sankara's commentaries on eleven principal Upanisads. We begin with the Isa Upanisad.

Though this is the smallest of all Upanisad with only 19 hymns, it incorporates almost every major doctrine of

Advaitism.   This would become clear from the following analysis.

The first two hymns of this Upanisad go as:

> *"Om. All this - whatsoever moves on the earth - should be covered by the Lord.   Protect (yourself) through that detachment.   Do not covet anybody's wealth.."* *[Stanza No: 1]*

> *"By doing Karma, indeed, should one wish to live here for a hundred years. For a man, such as you (who wants to live thus), there is no way other than this, whereby Karma may not cling to you."* *[Stanza No: 2]*

The Upanisads, it is well known, generally advocate Gyanayoga. But these verses seem to give a call in favour of Karmayoga. How does one explain this paradox?

Sankara resolves it by positing that the above injunction to engage in Karmayoga was applicable to only 'ignorant people', i.e. those who lacked the ability to differentiate the soul from the body. It would be recalled from Chapter 8 that Sankara looked upon Karmayoga as a means of self-purification and spiritual upliftment for the common man. It was deemed by him as the pathway to Gyanayoga. All those who lacked true knowledge were required to adhere to Karmayoga. We thus see that with the above-mentioned caveat added by Sankara, the foregoing verses indeed substantiate a basic tenet of Advaitism espousing Karmayoga for the vast majority, while at the same time not denying in any way that Gyanayoga constitutes the ultimate path to salvation.

Turning to stanza No: 6, it goes as:

"*They that deny the Self, return after death to a godless birth, blind, enveloped in darkness.*"

This is construed by Sankara by invoking the doctrine of Maya. He says one who denies the Self is indeed ignorant. In other words he is beguiled by Maya and hence undergoes transmigration. Advaitism regards human life as spelling nothing but unmitigated sorrow. This is why human birth has been described in this hymn in such sombre terms.

The stanzas 6 and 7 intone:

"*He who sees all beings in the Self itself, and the Self in all beings, feels no hatred by virtue of that (realization).*" [Stanza No: 6]

"*When to the man of realization all beings become the very Self, then what delusion and what sorrow can there be for that seer of oneness?*" [Stanza No: 7]

Sankara says that these two hymns portray a person who has attained supreme knowledge. To such a sage, Advaitism holds, there is no distinction between himself and others as he identifies himself with Brahman. (See Chapter IV.) This is the state of salvation when the enlightened Being no more experiences any sorrow, unhappiness, desires, etc. and remains immersed in an ocean of unalloyed bliss. He is naturally free from all negative emotions like envy, jealousy, etc. In Sankara's works one often comes across portrayals of a supreme sage couched in such terms. The above verses also say that an enlightened Being no more suffers from sorrow, jealousy, etc. and are therefore very much in conformity with Advaitism.

Turning now to the Ken Upanisad. This Upanisad focuses on exploring what constitutes the essence or core of man which upholds life. One comes across in it a number of hymns which are couched in analogous terms and which enquire as to what enables man to think, see, etc. One of these hymns is given below:

> *"Willed by whom does the directed mind go towards its objects? Being directed by whom does the vital force that precedes all, proceed (towards its duty)? By whom is this speech willed that people utter? Who is the effulgent being who directs the eye and the ears?"* [I. i]

This is answered as follows:

> *"That which man does not see with the eye, but thanks to which the eye can see, know that alone to be Brahman and not what people worship as an object."* [I. 7]

> *"That which man does not hear with the ear, but what makes hearing possible, know that to be Brahman and not this that people worship as an object".* [I. 8]

There are many such hymns in this Upanisad. They speak about Brahman as the essence of man which enables him to see, hear, think, etc. But at the same time these hymns say that Brahman is incorporeal and beyond sensory perceptions. Another hymn says that Brahman cannot be visualized by mind. Thus, Brahman is delineated in this Upanisad as incorporeal, ineffable, etc. while at the same time It is deemed as the very substratum of man sustaining his life. Surely, a better definition of Brahman could not be given by Advaitism.

The Ken Upanisad says that one who fails to recognize the true nature of Brahman has to undergo great suffering; but one who cognizes It attains immortality. This is put forth as:

> "If one has realized here, then there is truth; if he has not realized here, then there is great destruction. The wise ones, having realized (Brahman) in all beings and having turned away from this world, become immortal." [ll. 5]

The last line speaks of realization of Brahman on acquiring supreme knowledge. When this happens, man never gets birth again. This is described by the hymn as attainment of immortality. Everybody else is subject to birth and death when he suffers the agonies of the world. This is what the first line refers to. These concepts are very much in conformity with Advaitism. It too stipulates that only an enlightened Being gets liberated from the unending cycle of births and deaths, while all others remain shackled by it and have as their lot nothing but sorrow.

Turning now to the Katha Upanisad.

This Upanisad seeks answer to a question which has

intrigued man since aeons: What happens to man after death? This query is posed as follows:

> *"This doubt that arises, consequent on the death of a man - some saying It exists, and others saying It does not exist - I would know this, under your instruction. Of all the boons, this one is the third boon."* *[I. i. 20]*

It is being enquired whether there exists any entity like Soul having eternal existence which outlives the destruction of the body. In response, the Upanisad introduces a key metaphysical concept, namely, what is impermanent cannot lead to what is permanent. The attribute of permanence is thus very much extolled. The reader will recall that this concept implicitly forms the central plank of Advaitism too. (See Chapters 4 & 5.)   This is why permanence is associated in Advaitism solely with Brahman, the only Reality. That impermanence can never lead to permanence is affirmed as follows:

> *"Since I know this treasure is impermanent - for that permanent entity cannot be attained through impermanent things..."* *[I. ii . 10]*

But then what is permanent in the world? This is nothing but the Soul which is characterized as follows:

> *"The intelligent Self is neither born nor does It die. It did not originate from anything, nor did anything originate from It.   It is birthless, eternal, undecaying, and ancient. It is not killed even when the body is destroyed."* *[I. ii 18]*

Surely, Advaitism will wholly concur with the above depiction of Soul. (See Chapter IV.)

Advaitism postulates the immanence of Brahman as well as the fact that It is partless and undifferentiated. This is affirmed as follows in this Upanisad:

> *"What is indeed here, is there, what is there, is here likewise. He who sees as though there is difference here, goes from death to death." [ll. i. 10]*

> *"This is to be attained through the mind indeed. There is no diversity here whatsoever. He who sees as though there is difference here, goes from death to death." [ll. i. 10]*

These hymns basically proclaim that the cosmos is devoid of any differences or differentiation, and reject the existence of any diversity in it. They thus very much substantiate the basic Advaitic dogma that there is nothing but non-dual Brahman which is characterized by partlessness and uniformity.

Similarly, the Advaitic notion that the empirical world is only an apparent transformation of Brahman is expressed as follows:

> *"Just as fire, though one, having entered the world, assumes separate forms in respect of different shapes, similarly, the Self inside all*

*beings, though one, assumes a form in respect of
each shape; and (yet) It is outside." [ll. ii. 9]*

Finally, the crucial Advaitic doctrine of Maya is
formulated in this Upanisad, though in an implicit way as
follows:

*"Just as the sun, which is the eye of the whole
world, is not tainted by the ocular and external
defects, similarly, the Self, that is but one in all
beings, is not tainted by the sorrows of the
world, It being transcendental." [ll. ii. 11]*

It is thus implied that what goes on in this world does
not tarnish the sublimity of Brahman or Self. The world is also
implicitly envisaged as a projection of Self or Brahman. But
this is precisely what Sankara has always contended, arguing
that since the world of Maya is a mere superimposition on
Brahman, the former in no way can impinge on the latter.

We now turn to Taittiriya Upanisad. In its very
beginning we come across an interesting description of Soul:

*"In the space that there is in the heart, is this
person who is realizable through knowledge, and
who is immortal and effulgent." [I. vi. 1-2]*

Here the immortality and effulgence of Soul are
highlighted. This is how Advaitism also characterizes It.
Moreover, it is said that Soul can be realized through
knowledge (alone) which is synonymous with Gyanamarg.
This is again a central tenet of Advaitism.

Another verse in this Upanisad says inter-alia:

> *"I am like that pure realty (of the Self), which is in the sun... and I am immortal and undecaying." [I. X. 1]*

The identification of Self with the sun betokens identity of Soul with Brahman. The allusion to the Soul being immortal and undecaying signifies Its eternal existence and immutability. The reader will readily perceive that the above description of Soul will be fully substantiated by Advaitism.

In this Upanisad, one comes across a clear-cut injunction asking man to engage in worldly duties. This goes as:

> *"Having taught the Vedas, the preceptor imparts this post-instruction to the students: 'Speak the truth. Practise righteousness. Make no mistake about study. Having offered the desirable wealth to the teacher, do not cut off the line of progeny. There should be no inadvertence about truth. There should be no deviation from righteous activity. There should be no mistake about protecting yourself. Do not neglect propitious activities. Do not be careless about learning and teaching...." [I. XI. 1]*

Sankara fully concurs with this passage and construes it as a call for observance of Karmayoga by the common man. It will be recalled from Chapter 8 that Sankara deemed Karmayoga as mandatory for everybody except for that rare individual who possessed the ability to differentiate body from Soul. The above passage exhorting the common man to discharge his worldly duties thus very much conforms to advocacy of Karmayoga by Sankara for all those who are under the spell of Maya.

Towards the end of this Upanisad one comes across a description of an enlightened sage. This goes as:

> *"The enlightened man is not afraid of anything after realizing that Bliss of Brahman, failing to reach which, words turn back along with the mind. Him, indeed, this remorse does not afflict: 'Why did I not perform good deeds, and why did I perform bad deeds? He who is thus enlightened attains the Self with which these two are identical; for it is he, indeed, who knows thus, who can realize the Self which these two really are. This is the teaching."* [ll. ix. 1]

These lines could have been drafted by Sankara himself. Here Brahman is identified with bliss. The expression "(from) which words turn back" reflects Its ineffability and indescribability. It will be readily recalled that this is how Brahman is characterized in Advaitism. Moreover, the enlightened sage is described in this hymn as free of any mental agitation, as above good and bad. But this is precisely how Advaitism too visualizes enlightenment. An enlightened sage having identified himself with the cosmos necessarily rises above all temporal considerations, both good and bad, and nothing can disturb the utter equanimity of his mind.

Turning now to the Mundaka Upanisad:

Advaitism looks upon Brahman as the Sole Reality beyond which there is nothing to apprehend or realize. Everything in the world therefore becomes known once Brahman is cognized. One finds this central tenet of Advaitism clearly enunciated in following two hymns of Mundaka Upanisad in the form of a question and answer:

> *"Saunaka, well known as a great householder, having approached Angiras duly, asked, 'O adorable sir, (which is that thing) which having been known, all this becomes known?"* [l. i. 3]

The reply goes as:

> *"(By the higher knowledge) the wise realize everywhere that which cannot be perceived and grasped, which is without source, features, eyes and ears, which has neither hands nor feet, which is eternal, multiformed, all-pervasive, extremely subtle, and undiminishing, and which is the source of all."* [l. i. 6]

The reader will readily observe that the above description of Brahman endowing It with immanence, incorporeality, immutability, etc., very much corresponds to Its portrayal in Advaitism.

Mundaka Upanisad brings out the inadequacy of rituals as follows:

> *"The deluded fools, believing the rites inculcated by the Vedas and the Smrtis to be highest, do not*

understand the other thing (that leads to) liberation. They, having enjoyed (the fruits of actions) in the abode of pleasure on the heights of heaven, enter this world or an inferior one." [l. ii 10]

No doubt, this is something with which Advaitism will wholly concur. Advaitism looks upon rituals as a part of Karmayoga; they can lead to man's self-purification but could never achieve salvation by themselves.

In this Upanisad one finds the Guru being commended as follows:

"To him who has approached duly, whose heart is calm and whose outer organs are under control, that man of enlightenment should adequately impart that knowledge of Brahman by which one realizes the true and imperishable Purusa." [l. ii. 13]

Sankara always insisted that receiving the Guru's guidance was a sine qua non for man's for spiritual progress. He invariably described the Guru as somebody who was enlightened and who had cognized the ultimate truth. The above Upanisadic hymn is therefore fully consistent with Sankara's visualization and role of a Guru.

We will now quote two hymns from this Upanisad which portray Brahman in a manner very much reminiscent of Its depiction by Sankara.:

"There the sun does no shine, nor the moon or the stars; nor do these flashes of lightening shine

there. How can this fire do so? Everything shines according as He does so; by His light all this shines diversely." [ll. ii. 10]

Sankara in Vivekachoodamani described Brahman as the light of all lights.

Another description of Brahman in this Upanisad goes as follows:

'All this that is in front is but Brahman, the immortal. Brahman is at the back, as also on the right and the left. It is extended above and below, too. This world is nothing but Brahman, the highest." [ll. ii. 11]

But this is nothing but the central dogma of Advaitism that non-dual Brahman is the sole Reality.

Finally, the central Advaitic doctrine of identity between Soul and Brahman finds expression in this Upanisad as follows:

"Two birds that are ever associated and have similar names, cling to the same tree. Of these, one eats fruits of varied tastes, and the other looks on without eating." [lll. I. 1]

"On the same tree, the individual soul remains entangled (i.e. stuck), as it were; and so it moans, being worried by its impotence. When it sees thus the other, the adored Lords, and His

glory, then it becomes liberated from sorrow."
[Ill. I. 2]

Advaitism construes these hymns as follows: The two birds alluded to in the first hymn are a metaphor for individual self and Brahman respectively. Under the impact of Maya, the individual self forgets its true nature and gets enmeshed in the affairs of the world. Hence there is the imagery of one bird eating fruits. As regards the bird who is desisting from eating, it clearly epitomizes the immutable Brahman. This hymn thus is very much based on a basic Advaitic dogma.

Turning now to the second hymn: as per Advaitism man or soul is essentially no different from Brahman. But it is thanks to ignorance created by Maya that what is One appears as Many. This is why the individual self mistakenly believes that it is different from Brahman. It therefore undergoes suffering. This is portrayed by the expression 'the soul moans'. But when true knowledge dawns, the soul becomes aware of its original form which is nothing but Brahman. It then experiences bliss and this state is visualized as 'liberation from sorrow'.

Turning now to the Mandukya Upanisad: There are a number of verses in it which describe Brahman in terms identical with those used by Advaitism. Cited below are some such verses:

"All this is surely Brahman. This Self is Brahman. The Self, such as It is, is possessed of four quarters." *[No: 2]*

"This one is the Lord of all; this one is Omniscient; this one is the inner Director (of all); this one is the Source of all; this one is verily the place of origin and dissolution of all beings." [No: 6]

These hymns basically put forth that there is nothing except Brahman, that It is omniscient, and is responsible for genesis and dissolution of the cosmos. Surely, Advaitism cannot but wholly concur with such a portrayal of Brahman.

We now turn to Aiteriya Upanisad. This Upanisad contains a detailed description as to how the Supreme Being created different creatures. But Advaitism holds that there is no creation. Sankara accounts for this apparent anomaly by portraying the world as a phantasm created by a magician. This magician is none other than the Supreme Being. But a phantasm has existence only so long as there is a magician and therefore it is looked upon as an illusion.

Sankara thus implies that just as in the case of a phantasm, the creation of the world cannot be deemed to be wholly real. Quoting from his gloss:

1

"Just as an intelligent juggler, who has no material, transforms himself, as it were, into a second self ascending into space, similarly the omniscient and omnipotent Deity, who is a supreme magician creates Himself as another in the form of the universe. On this view, the schools that hold such beliefs as the unreality of

169

*both cause and effect have no legs to stand on
and are totally demolished."*

Turning now to Brahadarnyaka Upanisads: This
Upanisad contains a number of hymns which reiterate the
central dogma of Advaitism pertaining to the identity of Soul
with Brahman.   Some of them are adduced below:

> *"This (Self) was indeed Brahman in the
> beginning.   It knew only Itself as, 'I am
> Brahman'. Therefore, It became all." [I. iv. 10]*

> *"The Brahman ousts (slights) one who knows
> him as different from the Self.   The Ksatriya
> ousts one who knows him as different from the
> Self.   Worlds ousts one who knows them as
> different from the Self." [ll. iv. 6]*

This Upanisad is unique among the Upanisads in that it
contains an explicit reference to the unreality of the world. It
speaks of our variegated temporal world as if all the different
objects which we perceive in it were not in reality there.
Quoting from it:

> *"Because when there is duality, as it were, then
> one smells something, one sees something, one
> hears something. But when to the knower of
> Brahman everything has become the Self, then
> what should one smell and through what, what
> should one hear and through what, what should
> one speak and through what, what should one
> think and through what, what should one know*

and through what? Through what, O Maitreyi, should one know the knower? [ll. iv. 14]

The above passage implies that the cosmos in truth is undifferentiated and totally devoid of differences. The world around us is clearly held to be less than real. Surely, this is nothing but an enunciation of the Advaitic doctrine of Maya.

We have now finished our review of principal Upanisads. It would be clear from it that these Upanisads not only concur with Advaitism but also put forth its basic dogmas, though implicitly and indirectly. Moreover, it is also evident that many Upanisadic hymns cannot be properly understood outside the framework of Advaitism, especially without invoking the doctrine of Maya.

Thus, we can confidently conclude that Sankara was fully justified in affirming that his writings were totally in conformity with what Upanisads propounded.

1.   *Eight Upanisads with commentary of Sankaracarya. Volume ll. Translated by Swami Gambhirananda. Advaita Ashrama. Publication Department. 5, Delhi. Entally Road, Calcutta - 700014. Page 22*

"*Although the creation of this sphere of the universe appears to us to be a stupendous task, yet to God it is a mere pastime, because His power is infinite. Even though people may fancy that sport also as some subtle motive behind it, still no motive can be thought of here, since the Vedas declare that He has all desires fulfilled. Again, there can be neither inactivity, nor any mad activity, since there are the Vedic texts about creation and omniscience.*" [*From Sankara Bhashyam.*]

Chapter 12

The Sankara Bhashyam: Sankara's crowning glory

We are going to review in this chapter what is indubitably the most renowned and abstruse of Sankara's works, namely, Sankara Bhashyam which is his commentary on Brahma-Sutras, a major scripture of Hinduism. But before we turn to the analysis of Sankara Bhashyam it would be in order to say a few words about Brahma-Sutras.

Brahma Sutras is counted among the three most important scriptures of Hinduism, the other two being the Upanisads and the Gita. It represents the essence of Upanisads. The entire text comprises nothing else than 555 pithy aphorisms, each of which consists of only five or six words.

Most of these aphorisms by themselves do not make much sense due to their extreme brevity. They can be made meaningful only by adding a few appropriate words to them; sometimes the number of words inserted for clarification exceeds the number of words in the original aphorism.

Thanks to the extraordinary succinctness and inherent ambiguity of various aphorisms, Brahma-Sutras have proved a fertile source for varied and conflicting interpretations by different commentators. Each commentator naturally claimed that this text conformed to the school of metaphysics propounded by him.

Sankara was the first savant to write a detailed Bhashyam on Brahma-Sutras. The word 'Bhashyam' in this chapter will henceforth connote Sankara's Bhashyam on Brahma-Sutras unless otherwise specified. Sankara basically focuses on bringing out in this Bhashyam the following:

(i)   How Brahma-Sutras substantiates Advaitism

(ii)   How other systems of philosophy like Samkhyaism then prevalent were not consistent with Brahma-Sutras.

Significantly enough, in Sankara Bhashyam one comes across elucidation of many aspects of Advaitism which is not found elsewhere in Sankara's writings. A detailed study of this Bhashyam is therefore a must for any serious student of Advaitism.

Sankara asserts emphatically in this Bhashyam that the Upanisads provide the only true source of knowledge. He thus implicitly rejects other non-Vedantic systems of philosophy then in vogue. He declares that all the Upanisads agree with each other in essence. He bases this conclusion on the following aphorism in Brahma-Sutras:

"Because the knowledge (gathered from the various Upanisads) is the same (as regards consciousness being the cause). [B. S. I. i. 10]

It needs to be mentioned here that the words in the

bracket do not belong to the original aphorism and have been inserted to bring out its meaning. We will follow the above convention throughout this chapter, i.e. the words in the bracket will invariably connote the addition made for clarification. The reader will also observe that if these additional phrases are not introduced the aphorism will be devoid of meaning. This holds true for most of the aphorisms in Brahma-Sutras as will become evident from the perusal of what follows.

To establish how Brahma-Sutras endorses Advaitism, Sankara asserts that the delineation of Brahman in it tallies with Its characterization by Advaitism. He affirms that Brahma-Sutras ascribes to Brahman the attributes of creatorship of the universe, omniscience, as well as being an epitome of bliss. Sankara cites following aphorisms in Brahma-Sutras to substantiate this conclusion:

> *"That (is Brahman) from which (are derived) the birth etc., of this (universe)."* [B. S. I. i. 2]

> *"(Brahman is omniscient) because of (Its) being the source of the scriptures."* [B. S. I. i. 3]

> *"The Blissful One (is the Supreme Self) on account of repetition."* [B.S.I.i.12]

As is well known, the premise of identity of cause and effect constitutes a central plank of Advaitism. Sankara asserts that this is also upheld by Brahma-Sutras, and in support of this contention adduces the following aphorism:

> *"(The pre-existence and non-difference of the effect are established) from reasoning and other Upanisadic texts."* [B.S. II. i. 18]

This dogma constitutes a basic tenet of Advaitism because it posits that the Absolute Reality (cause) and the temporal world (effect) are one and the same. It is from this premise that the doctrine of Maya naturally emerges. (See Chapters IV and V.)

Sankara acknowledges that the cause and the effect may differ in terms of appearance, form, etc., but contends that such differences do not impugn upon the essential identity of the two. He elaborates this aspect in his Bhashyam as follows:

1

> *"A thing does not become different just because of the appearance of some peculiarity; for Devadatta, even though noticed in different attitudes when he has his hand and feet contracted or extended, does not differ in his personality, since the recognition of identity persists as, It is he himself."*

Sankara thus elegantly illustrates how our multi-faceted changing world is in essence identical with undifferentiated immutable Brahman and how the apparent differences between them are to be regarded as superficial.

Sankara also points out that the Upanisads too uphold the above doctrine of non-difference between cause and effect. Here he quotes the following Upanisadic hymn:

> *"As, O amiable one, all things made of clay are known when a lump of clay is known, since a modification has speech as its origin and exists only in name; as clay alone it is true."* *[Ch. VI. i.4]*

Sankara in this way demonstrates how the dogma of identity of cause and effect is embraced by the Upanisads and Brahma-Sutras.   It is thus established how this basic tenet of Advaitism is fully endorsed by these two major scriptures.

In the Upanisads Brahman is described in two mutually contradictory ways: as devoid of human attributes, and as possessing them.   In Sankara Bhashyam it is explicitly stipulated that it is the portrayal of Brahman as transcendent, as delinked from the temporal world, which supersedes Its other depictions ascribing human attributes to It.   One does not come across a categorical assertion of this kind in Sankara's other works. Moreover, it is only in the Sankara Bhashyam that Sankara proffers an explanation as to why in some places the Upanisads portray Brahman as possessing attributes even though this is not Its real nature.   Sankara asserts that human features are associated with Brahman to enable Its worship by man.

These two themes i.e. the essentially transcendent character of Brahman as well as ascribing anthropomorphic attributes to It to enable man to worship It, have been elucidated by Sankara as follows in his Bhashyam:

2

> *"Hence in sentences of this kind, the formless Brahman alone, just as it is spoken of by the texts themselves, has to be accepted. But the other texts, speaking of Brahman with form, have the injunction about meditations as their main objectives. So long as they do not lead to some contradiction, their apparent meaning should be accepted. But when they involve a*

contradiction, the principle to be followed for deciding one or the other is that, those that have the formless Brahman as their main purport are more authoritative than the others which have not that as their main purport. It is according to this that one is driven to the conclusion that Brahman is formless and not its opposite, though texts having both the purports are in evidence."

Sankara cites the following aphorism from Brahma-Sutras to show how this text concurs with the above viewpoint:

"Not even according to place can Brahman have a two-fold characteristic for everywhere (It is thought to be without attributes)." [B.S. III. ii. 11]

But then why is Brahman portrayed in different ways in the Upaniṣads? Brahma-Sutras says:

"And like light, (Brahman) can (be assumed to have different appearances) so that (the scriptures) may not become purportless." [B.S.III.ii.15]

The implication of the above aphorism as brought out by Sankara is as follows: It is a common experience that light seems to assume different forms depending upon the object on which it falls, though in reality its basic nature remains unchanged. In the same way this aphorism figuratively conveys that the attributeless Brahman sometimes appears as if endowed with human features. Moreover, the aphorism also posits that if Brahman had not so appeared (i.e. as possessing human attributes), Its worship by man would have proved an impossibility. This is signified by the expression "scriptures may not become purportless".

We thus see how Brahma-Sutras and Advaitism agree that Brahman is essentially transcendent and Its portrayals endowing It with human features are of secondary importance.

In Sankara Bhashyam one finds answers to a number of crucial queries regarding the nature of Brahman, and these include:

i.   Why did Brahman create the world? Was there any purpose behind it?

ii.   No person can perform anything without bodily organs. Does Brahman possess a body?

iii.   No person can build or construct anything without instruments. How did Brahman create the universe without any accessories?

iv.   Brahman surely undergoes transformation as a result of creating the cosmos. How could one then regard It as immutable?

v.   How could Brahman, which is an epitome of purity and sublimity, create a world which abounds with misery and sorrow?

One does not find similar questions being raised in any of Sankara's other works.

The queries numbered (ii) and (iii) raise a doubt as to how attributeless Brahman could create the world, though it is devoid of organs, accessories, etc. Similarly, the query at number IV expresses bewilderment because Brahman remains unaffected, even though It is engaged in the process of creation. By thus assuming the role of a Devil's advocate, Sankara is subjecting to scrutiny Advaitism's basic assumption regarding the nature of Brahman i.e. It being without attributes and Its immutability.

Sankara argues that such questions are intrinsically invalid because Brahman differs radically from the physical world as the latter is apprehended by our senses. The laws of our physical universe are therefore not at all applicable to It. Sankara emphasizes the need to accept whatever the Upanisads postulate regarding the nature of Brahman and not to subject it to the so-called logical scrutiny.

He says in his Bhashyam:

3

> *"There is no violation of the texts about partlessness, since partlessness is accepted on account of its very "mention" in the Upanisads", and the Upanisads are the only authority about It, but not so are the senses, etc. Hence It has to be accepted just as It is presented by the Upanisads. The Upanisads prove both the facts for Brahman – the non – transformation of Brahman as a whole and partlessness. Even the things of this world like gems, incantations, herbs and so on, are seen to possess many powers capable of producing incompatible effects under the influence of a*

variety of space (environment), time and cause. And even these powers can be known not from mere reasoning but from such instruction as, "such a thing has such kinds of potency with the aid of such things, on such thing, and for such purposes". So what need has one to argue that the nature of Brahman, whose power is beyond all thought, cannot be ascertained unless it be through the Vedas."

As regards the first query (i.e. why Brahman created the world), Sankara looks upon world's creation as Brahman's sport. The oft-raised objection that the Supreme Being could not have possibly produced the world in a frivolous manner as such a happening would conflict with His sublimity is rebutted by Sankara is as follows:

4

"Although the creation of this sphere of the universe appears to us to be a stupendous task, yet to God it is a mere pastime, because His power is infinite. Even though people may fancy that sport also has some subtle motive behind it, still no motive can be thought of here, since the Vedas declare that He has all desires fulfilled. Again, there can be neither inactivity, nor any mad activity, since there are Vedic texts about creation and omniscience."

Sankara bases the above gloss on following aphorism:

"But (creation for Brahman is) a mere pastime like what is seen in the world."   [B.S. ll. I. 33]

Finally, turning to the last and fifth query, Sankara reconciles the existence of sublime Brahman with that of our highly imperfect world as follows. He gives the simile of cow-dung giving rise to scorpions. Thus, he illustrates how the source of creation need have no similarity with what is created (as has happened in case of Brahman and the world). Sankara basically relies on the doctrine of Maya to elucidate how non-dual immutable Brahman could appear like our multi-faceted world. He points out that the world being a creation of Maya is not on the same level of reality as Brahman. He characterizes the world's diversity and variegated form as an illusion arising out of ignorance. Quoting from his Bhashyam:

5

> *"(There is no incompatibility involved between the Brahman and the world) since it is admitted that this difference of aspects is created by ignorance. For a thing does not become multi-formed just because it is so imagined through ignorance. Not that the moon, perceived to be many by man with blurred vision (timira-diplopia), become really so. Brahman becomes subject to all kinds of (phenomenal) actions like transformation, on account of the differences of aspects, constituted by name and form, which remain either differentiated or non-differentiated, which cannot be determined either as real or unreal, and which are imagined through ignorance."*

In an analogous way Advaitism sheds light on a similar enigma: how to account for sufferings of the human body when it is the seat of pure Self? It will be recalled here that

Advaitism has consistently drawn a sharp line of demarcation between immutable Brahman or Soul and the perishable human body. The difference between absolute Reality of Brahman and the relative Reality of the body is brought out in the Sankara Bhashyam as follows:

· 6

> *"As the light of the sun or moon spreads over the whole sky, and yet when it comes in contact with a conditioning factor like a finger etc., it seems to become straight or bent like them as these things become so, but not so in reality; or as space seems to move when pots etc., change place, but not so in reality; or as the reflection of the sun in a plate of water etc., seems to shake with the shaking of those things, but not so the sun that is the prototype; similarly even though a part of God, which is conjured up by nescience, conditioned by the intellect etc., and called an individual soul, suffers pain, still God, the possessor of that part, has no suffering."*

The above passage elucidates the basic Advaitic dogma that Soul or Brahman alone constitutes the true Reality. The human body or the world being a creation of Maya is a mere superimposition on It. This is why as per Advaitism it is a cardinal error to identify one's body with Soul as is normally done. Thus, one can in no way hold Brahman responsible for the sorrows and inequities of the world as the two belong to different levels of reality. Similarly, man's transgressions cannot be attributed to or associated with Soul.

Sankara as we have seen earlier was also a theist. In his Bhashyam, he reconciles God's omnipotence and sublimity with the gross imperfections of our world as follows:

7

> *"No fault attaches to God, since this unequal creation is brought about in conformity with the virtues and vices of the creatures that are about to be born. Rather, God is to be compared to rain. Just as rainfall is a common cause for the growth of paddy, barley, etc. the special reasons for the differences of paddy, barley, etc., being the individual potentiality of the respective seeds, similarly God is the common cause for the birth of gods, men, and others, while the individual fruits of works associated with the individual creatures are the uncommon causes for the creation of the differences among the gods, men, and others. Thus God is not open to the defects of partiality and cruelty, since He takes other factors into consideration."*

We saw earlier that Sankara exhorted observance of Karmayoga by the common man and considered it as the sole means of self-purification as well as of eradicating ignorance which being a manifestation of Maya prevents man from cognizing Reality. (See Chapter 8.) No doubt, one wonders how actions in this world of Maya can lead one to sublime Brahman. This is elucidated by Sankara with the help of following analogy. He says that what man sees in his dream often has correlation with his real life. Thus, an imaginary event gets linked to real life; in the same way actions in the domain of Maya have their impact on the transcendent Soul.

Quoting from the Bhashyam:

8

> *"In support of this (true result arising from an unreal basis) is the Vedic text: "If in the course of performing some rites with a view of obtaining results, one sees a woman in a dream, one should conclude from that dream that the rite will be successful", [Ch. V. ii. 8], which shows the true fulfillment of a desire from the seeing of a false dream."*

Advaitism identifies Soul with Brahman. But what kind of identity is this? The Soul after all resides in the tiny human body while Brahman is all-pervasive. Sankara resolves this paradox with the help of a simile as follows:

9

> *"And it is to be understood that this individual Soul is a reflection of the Supreme Self like the semblance of the sun in water. Not that the Soul is the Self Itself, nor is it something else. From this also it follows that just as when any one of the reflections of the sun moves, the other do not, similarly when any one individual Soul becomes associated with the result of its works, no other Soul is associated with it."*

The above passage is indeed very significant. It shows how transcendent entities like the Soul and Brahman cannot be categorized in terms of our corporeal world. This is why in Advaitism we come across what appear prima facie to be self-contradictory statements like Brahman and Soul are non-different yet not the same. Notably enough, the above gloss is based on the following aphorism of Brahma-Sutras:

> *"And (the individual Soul) is only a reflection (of the Supreme Self) to be sure."*   *[B.S. ll. iii. 50]*

Sankara's Bhashyam thus demonstrates how Brahma-Sutras fully endorses Advaitism. In particular, in the foregoing paragraphs we have shown how Brahma-Sutras posits following crucial Advaitic doctrines:

i.   That Brahman is an epitome of knowledge and bliss

ii.   Brahman is transcendent

iii.   The doctrine of identity of cause and effect.
       This implies that the world could not be different in essence from Brahman which is a central postulate of Advaitism.

iii.   Identity of Soul and Brahman.

Apart from establishing how Advaitism and Brahma-Sutras are fully in agreement, Sankara Bhashyam devotes considerable space to a discussion of various schools of metaphysics which were then in vogue. These include: Samkhyaism, Nyaya-Vaisesikaism, Mimamsakas, etc. The untenability of their doctrines is cogently brought out in this Bhashyam. In what follows we have briefly reviewed some of the arguments adduced by Sankara repudiating various schools of metaphysics.

We begin with Samkhyaism. This school of philosophy enjoyed immense respect around Sankara's times. This is borne out by the fact that among the earliest Hindu texts which were translated into Chinese in olden times, there were many which dealt with Samkhyaism. The ancient Chinese scholars obviously could have taken up only those texts for translation which were respected among the people. Sankara too acknowledges in his Bhashyam that the Samkhya doctrines and the sage Kapila, who formulated them, commanded much respect.

10

"But people generally depend for their enlightenment on the scriptures written by others. Being unable to comprehend the meaning of the Upanisads independently, they will turn to the Smrtis that have well-known authors, and they will comprehend the meaning of the Upanisads with their help; but they will not rely on our explanation, since the authors of the Smrtis command great respect."

"Besides, the Smrtis mention that Kapila and others had the (unobstructed prophetic) vision of seers. And there is the Upanisadic text, "(One should realize that God) who saw the seer Kapila emerging out in the beginning of creation and filled him with knowledge after his birth." [Sv. V 2]

Sankara also acknowledged that to some extent the Upanisads substantiated Samkhya doctrines. Samkhyaism like the Upanisads also holds that the cause and effect are identical. Similarly, Samkhyas also postulate the existence of an immanent principle in the cosmos (Prakriti), which is deemed to be incorporeal, eternal, self-existent, etc. It has been argued that the Prakriti of the Samkyas corresponds to the Absolute of the Upanisads since the two share some crucial characteristics like immanence, incorporeality, eternity, etc. Even Sankara acknowledges this commonality in his Bhashyam as follows:

11

> *"As the theory of Pradhana as the material cause of the universe approximates to the Vedantic philosophy; as it is supported by plausible reasons; and as it is accepted by some good followers of the Vedas."*

But, notwithstanding these areas of concord between Samkhyaism and Upanisads, it is indubitable that the former was in conflict with Advaitism.

This is because Samkhyaism presupposes existence of two independent entities, Purusha and Prakriti, and these cannot be reconciled with the monism of Advaitism. Sankara brings out the sharp dichotomy between Samkyaism and the Upanisads as follows:

He argues that the Prakriti of Samkhyas is insentient

while the Absolute of the Upanisads, if anything, is sentient.

¹²

> *"In the Upanisadic texts one cannot take one's stand on the insentient Pradhana imagined by the Samkhyas as the cause of the universe; for it is not presented in the Upanisads."*

He cites an aphorism from Brahma-Sutras which rejects Samkhyaism on the very same ground, i.e. insentience of Prakriti.

> *"(The Pradhana (Prakriti) of the Samkhyas) is not (the cause of the universe) because it is not mentioned in the Upanisads, (which fact is clear from the fact of) seeing."* [B. S. I. i. 5]

Sankara also contends that insentient Prakriti could not have possibly created our cosmos since it is characterized by immense diversity and complexity. He bases this reasoning on following aphorisms from Brahma-Sutras:

> *"The inferred one (Pradhana or Prakriti) is not (the cause) owing to the impossibility of explaining the design, as also for other reasons."* [B. S. II. i . 1]

> *"Even if (spontaneous modification of Pradhana be) accepted, still (Pradhana will not be cause) because of the absence of any purpose".* [B. S. II. i i . 6)

We thus see how Sankara clearly enunciates the arenas of discord between Vendanta and Samkhyaism and establishes how the latter was repudiated by Brahma-Sutras.

Another school of thought which held much sway around Sankara's period was that of Karmakanda. Proponents of this school called Mimamsakas attached overwhelming importance to performance of rituals. This was because they regarded the soul as the seer of man, and claimed that rituals alone could cleanse man of his sins. According to them, the primary objective of the Vedas was none else than to impart instructions regarding performance of various sacraments and rites. Punctilious engagement in ritualism by itself was considered adequate to achieve salvation. It was the soul and not God which was accorded the position of pre-eminence in this school. It was claimed by some Mimamsakas that the soul represented the Absolute of the Upanisads. In this way they essayed to reconcile their theology with Vedanta.

Sankara was totally opposed to the basic postulate of this school, namely, that rituals alone were enough to secure salvation. This is why in his writings he emphasizes any number of times the utter incompatibility between work (rituals) and knowledge.

Sankara's rebuttal of this basic premise of Mimamsakas ascribing pre-eminence to Soul and equating it with the Absolute goes as follows:

13

> *"These characteristic of transcendence etc., cannot logically apply to the embodied soul which identifies itself with the limitation*

imposed by name and form, conjured up by ignorance, and which imagines their attributes as its own. Hence Purusa (the conscious all-pervasive entity), met with in the Upanisads alone, is directly mentioned here."

He also cites two aphorisms from Brahma-Sutras repudiating Samkhyaism and the Karmakanda school as given below:

"(The entity), possessed of the qualities of not being seen etc., (is Brahman) for its characteristics are spoken of." [B. S. I. i i. 21]

"And the other two (i.e the individual soul and Prakriti) are not meant, for there is the mention of distinctive characteristics (of Brahman) and (its) differences (from the two)." [B. S. I. i i. 22]

Buddhism too had gained many adherents in early centuries of the Christian era. In Sankara's Bhashyam one comes across trenchant criticism of Buddhist doctrines. He rejects the doctrine of nihilism as follows:

14

"Moreover, non-existence can never be the source of anything, precisely because it is non-existence like the hare's horn etc. Were existence to arise out of non-existence, all the effects would be imbued with non-existence. But that goes against experience, for all things are perceived to exist as positive entities with their respective distinguishing features."

Buddhism denies that there exists anything which remains eternally immutable like Soul or Brahman; it holds that everything in the cosmos is marked by transitoriness, by continuous transformation. This is known as the doctrine of momentariness. Rejecting it, Sankara says:

15

> *"Moreover, when the nihilist asserts all things to be momentary, he will have to assert the perceiver also to be momentary. But that is an absurdity because of the fact of remembrance."*

> *"And why should not the nihilist be ashamed of himself when he holds on to the theory of momentariness at the same time that he recognizes all his perceptions from now on to the last breath and the past ones from his very birth till now as having happened to his own very same self?"*

During Sankara's times the idealist schools of Buddhism also held much sway. It was their basic contention that there is nothing truly real in the world around us and everything is a projection of mind. Sankara refutes this line-of-thought in most explicit terms as follows:

16

> *"As a matter of fact such things as a pillar, a wall, a pot, a cloth, are perceived along with each act of cognition. And it cannot be that the very thing perceived is non-existent. How can a man's words be acceptable, who while himself perceiving an external object through sense contacts still says, "I do not perceive, and that object does not exist", just as much as a man while eating and himself experiencing the*

satisfaction arising from that act might say,
"Neither do I eat, nor do I get any satisfaction?"

The above passage incidentally also illustrates that Sankara never regarded the temporal world as a pure Maya or a phantasmagoria as claimed by some of his critics.

1:    *Brahma Sutra Bhashyam of Adi Sankaracarya. Translation by Swami Gambhirananda. Advaita Ashram. ·5, Deli, Entally Road, Calcutta 700014. Page 343*
2:    *Ibid. Page 612*
3:    *Ibid. Page 355*
4:    *Ibid. Page 361*
5:    *Ibid. Page 356*
6:    *Ibid. Page 511*
7:    *Ibid. Page 363*
8:    *Ibid. Page 331*
9:    *Ibid. Page 515*
10:    *Ibid. Pages 300 & 301*
11:    *Ibid. Page 323*
12:    *Ibid. Page 47*
13:    *Ibid. Page 143*
14:    *Ibid. Page 415*
15:    *Ibid. Page 412*
16:    *Ibid. Pages 418 & 419*

"When once the Soule has lost her way, O then, how restlesse do's she stray! And having not her God for light, How do's she erre in endlesse night!"   [Robert Herrick.]

Chapter 13

Sankara - The Great Synthesizer.

We have analysed in previous chapters various facets of Sankara's philosophy. We are going to bring out in this chapter how Sankara absorbed elements from various theologies then in vogue, and fused them together into a harmonious and coherent system.

It hardly needs to be said that Advaitism primarily derives inspiration from the Upanisads and the Gita. But at the same time it shows a strong imprint of other schools of thought like Samkhyaism, Sramanism, Buddhism, etc., which were prevalent around Sankara's times. This is especially noteworthy as some of the tenets of these schools were sharply criticized and rejected by Sankara. Moreover, all of them repudiated the authority of the Upanisads.

Notwithstanding all this, Advaitism exhibits a degree of commonality with other rival theologies which is undoubtedly a testimony to Sankara's eclectic approach and to the breath of his vision. One can truly say without fear of being accused of over simplification that if one analyses Sankara's teachings in totality, one would find that almost every key doctrine of it has an analogue in some concept or other which was formulated earlier. This is why we have entitled this chapter as: 'Sankara - The Great Synthesizer'.

As we mentioned in Chapter III, when Sankara appeared on the scene, the Indian philosophical thought was indeed characterized above all by diversity and incoherence. Nobody suspected the common substratum lying below the superficially conflicting currents of thought. It needed an individual of Sankara's genius to identify this substratum and to make it the basis of a new, well-formulated system of philosophy, which later came to be known as "Advaitism".

The task facing Sankara was no doubt uninvidious. On every major issue, whether pertaining to metaphysics, cosmology, ritualism or even perspective towards life, there was a sharp divergence in opinions as put forth by various holy texts. As elucidated in Chapter III, the main Hindu scriptures i.e. the Vedas, the Upanisads and the Gita, far from presented a unified system of theology. The Upanisads spoke in different, and often in mutually contradictory, voices as regards even the basic tenets of metaphysics like nature of the Absolute, the relationship between soul and Brahman, the mode of genesis of the cosmos, etc. Similarly, they did not put forth any consistent viewpoint as regards a number of other crucial issues, such as the role of ritualism in man's spiritual life, whether embracing monasticism was essential to attain salvation, and so on. The Gita similarly incorporated disparate views and in no way resolved the ambiguities thrown up by the Upanisads. Moreover, to add to the confusion, the other schools of philosophy set forth doctrines which were often sharply at variance with what the Upanisads and the Gita propounded.

In this medley of theologies and jumble of doctrines, what was apparent to the eye was only the total absence of even a single unifying thread. Thus, ambiguity and lack of cohesion had come to dominate the Indian metaphysics for many centuries prior to Sankar's era. Dr. Radhakrishnan has portrayed the utter disarray which characterized metaphysical thought in India around Buddha's time as follows:

1

> *"A congeries of conflicting theories and guesses, accepted by some and denied by others, changing with man, reflecting the individual characters, emotions and wishes of their authors, filled the air. There were no admitted facts or principles which all recognized, but only dissolving views and intuitions. Discussions were ripe about the finiteness or infiniteness, or neither or both, of the world and the self, and the distinction of truth and appearance, the reality of a world beyond, the continuance of the soul after death and the freedom of the will. Some thinkers identified mind and soul, others distinguished them from each other. Some held to the supremacy of God, others to that of man. Some argued that we know nothing about it; others flattered their audience with mighty hopes and confident assurances. Some were busy building elaborate metaphysical theories; others were equally busy demolishing them."*

We will first turn to metaphysics to see how Advaitism overlapped with other schools of philosophy. Apart from Vedanta, a number of schools of philosophy were prevalent during Sankara's times and these included: Buddhism, Samkhyaism, Nyaya-Vaisesikaism.

They had sharp differences with Vedanta in that they not only rejected the authority of the Upanisads, but did not even acknowledge the existence of Brahman or Soul.

But all these systems of philosophy embraced certain basic doctrines which were essentially identical, and these being:

i.   Doctrine of transmigration of soul

ii.   Law of Karma

iii.   Considering emancipation from the cycle of life and death as the summum bonum of life, and equating this state with supreme bliss

Notably enough, Sankara took as the basis of his Advaitic philosophy the aforesaid three crucial dogmas which were common to all the major systems of theology, including Vedanta, known until his time.   He considered them as self-evident axioms which needed no proof or substantiation. This is borne out by the fact that he made no attempt, whether in his original works or commentaries, to justify them. Advaitism thus takes as its foundation the quintessence of various schools of Hindu philosophy and hence the title of this chapter "Sankara: The Great Synthesizer".

Sankara not only borrowed elements from other theologies but synthesized and harmonized disparate teachings of Hindu scriptures and texts.   Advaitism in a way can be called the common denominator of various viewpoints encompassed by Hinduism. Sankara's greatness lies in the fact that he did not repudiate even those facets of Hinduism which prima facie ran counter to Advaitism. Sankara, for instance, fully accepted the doctrine of incarnation as well as endorsed idol-worship, though they seem to totally negate the central Advaitic dogma of attributeless Brahman. What is most remarkable, Sankara built the edifice of Advaitism which was marked by impeccable logic and unimpeachable consistency by fusing together ideas and concepts which were at variance with each other. This furnishes us with the most striking proof of his genius.

Sankara's ability to synthesize elements from different schools of philosophy can best be illustrated as follows. The main three doctrines of Advaitism can be defined as:

i.   The doctrine of non-dual Brahman, the sole Reality
ii.   Identity of Soul with Brahman
iii.   The doctrine of Maya

The first two are clearly derived from Vedanta while the third was probably inspired by Buddhism. Let us see this in more detail now.

The doctrine that there exists nothing but Brahman is substantiated in the Upanisads and the Gita by numerous hymns. We have cited below some of them:

> *"All this has That as its essence; That is the Reality; That is the Self; That thou art."* [Ch. VI. viii 7]
> *"And this all are the Self."* [Br. II. iv. 6]
> *"And this is but Brahman."* [Mu. II. ii. 11]

> *"All this is but the Self."*   *[Ch. VIII. xxv. 21]*
> *"There is no difference whatever in It."*   *[Br. IV. iv. 19]*
> *"That by which one sees the indestructible Reality in all beings, undivided in the divided, know that knowledge as Sattwic." [Gita. 18.20) (Also see verses: 8.20, 13.14)*

The doctrine of identity of Soul and Brahman is affirmed by the Upanisads and the Gita as follows:

> *"I am Brahman." [Br. I. iv. 10]*
> *"Thou are That." [Ch. VI. viii. 7]*
> *"I am the Self, O Arjuna, dwelling in the minds of all people." [Gita. X. 20]*
> *"This is your Self which is within all."   [Br. III. iv. I]*
> *"This is the Internal Ruler, your immortal Self." [Br. III. vii. 3-22]*
> *"He who sees Me everywhere, and sees everything in Me. he never becomes lost to Me, nor do I become lost to him. [Gita 6.30]*
> *"He sees, who sees the Supreme   Lord, remaining the same in all beings...."   [13.27]*
> *"Because he who sees the Lord, seated the same everywhere...." [13.28]*

It is thus seen that the above doctrine identifying Soul with Brahman which is a central postulate of Advaitism is substantiated by several hymns of the Gita and the Upanisads.

In fact, this postulate ensues as a natural corollary of Advaitism's central dogma that nothing exists except Brahman.

But what about God?   Hinduism basically revolves around His visualization as the creator, as the sustainer, as the overlord, as the epitome of love, mercy, etc. The God of Hinduism is, therefore, inextricably linked with our temporal world. On the other hand, Advaitism accords the pre-eminent status to Brahman which is totally divorced from our world. It is a testimony to Sankara's genius that he could felicitously incorporate the concept of God within the parameters of Advaitism.   How he does so would become clear from the following:

2

> "Since the believers in a changeless Brahman have a predilection for absolute unity, there will be no ruler and the ruled, so that the assertion that God is the cause (of the universe) will be contradicted.... "

> No, since that omniscience (of God) is contingent on the manifestation of name and form which are creations of ignorance and which constitute the seeds of the world..."

> "Name and form which constitute the seeds of the entire expanse of phenomenal existence, and which are conjured up by nescience, are, as it were, non-different from the omniscient God, and they are non-determinable either as real or unreal, and are mentioned in the Vedas and the Smrtis as the power, called Maya, of omniscient God, or as prakrti (primordial Nature)."

The above excerpt clearly establishes that the link

between Brahman and God is through Maya. Moreover, it is Maya that brings into existence the empirical world, including the individual souls in human beings. The souls merely imagine themselves to be ruled by an omnipotent God, when in truth there are neither the individual souls nor the God. While the God and souls are essentially non-different from Brahman, they assume (seemingly) vastly different appearances within the ambit of our phenomenal world which is itself a creation of Maya.

> 3
>
> *"Thus like space conforming to the conditioning factors like pot, jar, etc., God conforms to the limiting adjuncts-name and form-created by nescience. And within the domain of empirical existence, He rules it over the selves which identify themselves with the (individual) intellects and are called creatures, and which though identical with Himself, conforms, like the spaces in pots etc., to the assemblages of bodies and senses created by name and form that are called up by nescience. Thus God's rulership, omniscience and omnipotence are contingent on the limiting adjuncts conjured up by nescience; but not so in reality can such terms as "the ruler", "the ruled", "omniscience", etc., be used with regard to the Self shining in Its own nature after the removal of all limiting adjuncts through illumination."*

We thus see how Sankara successfully fused together and harmonized conflicting concepts of God and Brahman.

As regards the all-important Advaitic doctrine of Maya, it was far from being an innovation which Sankara had introduced on his own in metaphysics.   As seen earlier (see Chapter III), the question of "reality" of the world had become a part of metaphysical speculation in India right since the time of Buddha.   The idealist schools of Buddhism went to the extent of depicting the phenomenal world as a projection of mind.

Thus, the notion that the phenomenal world was less than real had become firmly established by the early centuries of the Christian era when the idealist schools of Buddhism flourished.   Subsequently, these concepts were further developed by Gaudapada who linked true reality with immutability and unreality with change and flux. He could therefore posit that the phenomenal world was a creation of Maya.   This was the genesis of the doctrine of Maya which was to become the centre-piece of Advaitism.

Sankara culled out the doctrine of non-dual Brahman from Vedanta and connected it with the doctrine of Maya; these two doctrines came to constitute the twin pillars of Advaitism.

Incidentally, it may be mentioned here that even the term Advaitism was not coined by Sankara. A scholar says:

4

> *"The term 'advaita' is not one which was originally coined by the Jains, and so Samantabhadra (a Jain savant) must have adopted it from some other theory current in philosophical circles before him.   Therefore we are led to the conclusion that the term 'advaita'*

We thus see that Sankara was indeed heavily indebted to Vedanta and Gaudapada. But this should cause no surprise. Sankara repeatedly affirmed that he looked upon the panisads as the only authoritative source of knowledge while he considered Gaudapada as his Guru's Guru.   But what is remarkable, he borrowed ideas from schools of philosophy like Samkhyaism which he repudiated.   Some of the parallels between Samkhyaism and Advaitism are sketched below:

The doctrine of transmigration says that the soul moves from body to body and what happens to it during any incarnation depends crucially on how it had conducted itself in the previous one. But the soul by definition is immutable. How does it then carry the experiences of one birth to another?   Samkhyas posit that the soul is encapsulated at the time of death by a subtle body called "Lingsarira" in which all the data about the previous life is stored. This subtle body moves along with the soul and acts as a conduit for information from one life to another.   Quoting here from Dr. S. Radhakrishnan:

5

"Every ego possesses within the gross material body, which suffers dissolution at death, a subtle body formed of the psychical apparatus, including the senses.   This subtle body is the basis of rebirth, as well as the principle of personal identity in the various existences.

The subtle body, which retains the trace of all our experiences, is called the linga, or the mark distinguishing the purusa. The lingas are the empirical characteristics without which the different purusas cannot be distinguished."

Sankara too subscribes to a very analogous concept. He describes the subtle body surrounding the soul as "Sukshmasarira". Quoting from his Bhashyam on Brahma-Sutras:

6

"And that fire along with the other elements, which constitutes a habitat for the soul emerging out of its present body, must be subtle in nature and measure. It is thus that we gather from the Upanisadic declaration about its going out through the nerves that fire (as also the other element) is a subtle element. It is possible for it to move through the nerves because of its minuteness in size, and it is unobstructed because of its fineness by nature. It is because of this fact again that it is not perceived by people near when it departs from the body.

For this very reason, just because it is subtle, the other body, 'the subtle body', is not destroyed, even when the gross body is destroyed through cremation, etc."

Samkhyaism holds that there is no real bondage for Purusha. This is for the simple reason that Purusha is inherently pure and sublime; being immutable it retains these characteristics through eternity. This rules out the possibility of it ever being shrouded by ignorance, or being ever entrapped in a state of bondage. But Samkhyas also speak of bondage and liberation of Purusha. They circumvent this apparent anomaly by positing that the bondage of Purusha in truth is a mere illusion, and arises merely due to its proximity to Chitta (or consciousness). This is elucidated by giving the metaphor of reflection of the moon in a moving stream of water. Though the moon is stationary, it appears to be moving; in the same way, immutable Purusha catches its own reflection in Chitta (the pure component of Prakriti), and thus falls into the illusion that it is undergoing various experiences. Samkhyaism therefore clearly implies that man's so-called involvement in the world has no real basis. Incidentally, Sankara too cites the above metaphor in his Bhashyam on the verse 15.7 of the Gita which is obviously indicative of the linkage between Samkhyaism and Advaitism.

Surely, the reader is reminded here of Advaitism. Sankara too holds that the immutable Soul merely imagines itself as the experiencer, as the doer, etc. It acquires such misapprehensions due to its proximity to Buddhi or consciousness.

Dr. S. Radhakrishnan brings out this analogue as follows:

7

"The Samkhya account of Purusa and Jiva resembles in many respects the Advaita Vedanta account of the atman and the individual ego. The atman, according to the Advaita Vedanta, is free from action, from the encumbrances of body and mind which involve

us in action. The atman seems to act on account of its accidents. The unconditioned purusa (of Samkhyaism) or atman (of Advaitism) is regarded as Jiva, when it is confused with the narrow bounds of individuality. Strictly speaking, individuality belongs to the Suksmasarira in the Advaita and the lingasarira in the Samkhya. Vijnanabhiksu speaks of a mutual reflection, which is to some extent akin to the pratibimbavada of the Vedanta, which holds that the atman is reflected in the antahkarana, or the inner organ. The cidabhasa, or appearance of cit (as envisaged by Samkhyas), is the individual self or Jiva."

We thus see that Samkhyaism and Advaitism indeed shared a certain congruence of outlook vis-a-vis some crucial metaphysical concepts as brought out in foregoing paragraphs. There is overlapping between them in other arenas too.

Samkhyas took a pessimistic view of life. Here they continued the tradition established by Sramanas who too looked upon life as devoid of any import. Samkhyas denigrated ritualism and considered knowledge as the only means of securing enlightenment. Incidentally, they fully concurred in this regard with Buddhism. We find all these elements reflected in Gaudapada's Karika which later on left its vivid imprint on Sankara's Advaitism.

Finally, Samkhyaism attached much weightage to reasoning and logic. Sankara too similarly emphasized the importance of empirical observations. He held that in case of a conflict between one's perceptions and what is enunciated in the Vedas, the former should be given preponderance.

Apart from Samkhyaism, Advaitism also drew inspiration from other schools of philosophy as explained below:

Advaitism looks upon life as nothing but a source of sorrow and unmitigated misery. This is because true bliss is associated by it only with Brahman, the Sole Reality, and hence Advaitism lays so much stress on attainment of salvation or securing liberation from the cycle of life and death. (See Chapter IV.)   But what is noteworthy is the fact that the above concept, namely, that the temporal world can only yield misery and anguish is traceable to an ancient school of philosophy called Sramanism which was pravalent in India well before the dawn of the Christian era. Discerning no purpose whatsoever in worldly life, Sramanas called for severing of all links with it and embracing of monasticism.   It is easy to see that these notions later on indeed became an integral and crucial part of Advaitism.

To give another instance of impact of non-Vedantic schools of philosophy on Advaitism:

Sankara attached profound importance to meditation and advocated it as a means of obtaining salvation. However, one hardly finds any references to meditation and its role in achieving man's spiritual elevation in the Vedanta.   Here Sankara clearly drew inspiration from the school of Yoga which had become well established by early centuries of the Christian era.

It is thus clear that as far as metaphysics was concerned, Sankara very much played a synthesizing role, adapting elements from different theologies and blending them together in a seamless web.

Let us now turn to another important facet of religion, namely, ritualism.   How important are rituals in man's spiritual odyssey? This was an issue on which there was no consensus among various texts of Hinduism.   The Vedas, especially the Brahmana texts which were composed at a later stage, very much advocated ritualism.   In Sankara's times an influential denomination called Mimamsakas had spread which held that rituals alone could lead man to salvation. They went to the extent of giving a subservient position to God Himself. (See Chapter XII.)   As regards the Upanisads and   the Gita, these texts certainly do not ascribe any particular significance to ritualism.   We thus see that the main scriptures of Hinduism were sharply at variance with each other as far as ritualism was concerned.

Coming to later times, after the dawn of the Christian era an entirely new mode of divine worship, namely, idolatry had entered into Hinduism.   A large number of temples had been constructed and many superstitious practices had come into vogue. Moreover, different groups of people worshipped different gods, forgetting that there is only one Supreme Being.   Vaishnavites and Saivites especially looked upon each other with askance and rejected the notion that there could possible be any commonality between these two deities.

Sankara as a proponent of attributeless Brahman and as an advocate of Gyanamarg could have been expected to repudiate idolatry. But not only he did not do so, but went to the extent of encouraging the building of temples. He regularly prayed before idols of various deities and wrote a large number of devotional hymns suffused with profound piety and love of God. He endowed various deities in his poetry with gross, corporeal features such as beauty, charm, strength, etc. He at the same time emphasized that all gods ultimately represented only one Supreme Being. He thus tried to bridge the chasm between worshippers of various deities.

Sankara looked upon rites as a means of self-purification. This will become amply clear from the following passage taken from his Bhashyam:

> *Objection:* "*But how can they seek to know the Self through such rites as the daily reading of the Vedas, for they do not·reveal the Self as the Upanisads do?*"

> *Reply: The objection does not hold, for the rites are a means of purification. It is only when the rites have purified them, those people, with their minds clean, can easily know the Self that is revealed by the Upanisads. As the Mundaka Upanisad say, 'But his mind being purified, he sees through meditation that Self which has no parts' (III. i. 8). The Smrti also says, "A man attains knowledge only when his evil work has been destroyed, etc.' (Mbh. XII. ccii. 9)*

> *Objection:* "*How do you know that the regular rites are for purification?*"

*Reply: From such Sruti texts as the following:
"He indeed sacrifices to the Self who knows."
"This particular part of my body is being
improved by that (rite).", etc. (S. XI. II. vi.
13). All the Smrtis too speak of rites as being
purificatory, as, for instance, the passage, 'The
forty-eight acts of purification.", etc (cf. Gau.
VIII. 22). The Gita also says, "Sacrifices,
charity and austerity are purifying to the
intelligent aspirant' (XVIII. 5) and "All these
knowers of sacrifices have their sins destroyed
by the sacrifices.: (IV 30) [SB. Br. up. IV. iv.
22]*

It may be recalled that the attributless Brahman is
described in many places in Upanisads as possessing
anthropomorphic features. Sankara accounts for such
portrayals by affirming that these were meant to facilitate
worship of the Absolute. (See Chapter XII.) He thus again
endorses ritualism.

Sankara also acknowledges that the presence of
omnipresent God could be more pronounced in some places
than in others. Quoting from his Bhashyam:

8

*"Even though the Supreme Lord transcends all
limitations, still there can be a spatial
limitation for the sake of (His) manifestation.
For the Supreme Lord does become manifest (in
His majesty) out of favour for his worshippers.
Or because He becomes specially manifest in
particular spots like the heart, which are the*

215

*places (pradesa) for His revelation, therefore
from the point of view of manifestation, the
text about spatial limitation is justifiable even
in the case of the supreme Lord. This is how
the teacher Asmarathya thinks."*

We thus see how Sankara elegantly reconciled conflicting opinions vis-a-vis ritualism. At one extreme he rejected the Mimamsakas' viewpoint that rituals were all in all and could lead to salvation by themselves. But he also acknowledged a role for rituals and deemed them as a means of spiritual elevation.

Finally, let us turn to the ideal way of life as envisioned by various texts of Hinduism as well as by different schools of philosophy. Here again there was a divergence of viewpoints.

There were basically two schools of thought. One held that monasticism was the ideal way of life and worldly life was devoid of any import. On the other hand, it was claimed by the other school that a householder, provided he led a righteous existence, could also attain the topmost ladder of spirituality. Let us see who were the proponents of these rival schools.

Sramanas, Samkhyas, and Buddhists generally decried worldly existence. In the Upanisads again it is monasticism which is extolled. On the other hand, in the Gita the basic thrust is on discharging of one's duty; it therefore clearly advocates involvement in worldly life. In the Puranas too one comes across numerous instances of householders having reached the pinnacle of spirituality as a result of leading a virtuous existence.

Thus, the basic question which remained unanswered was the following: What was preferable - Gyanamarg which called for embracing of monasticism or Karmamarg which of course presupposed involvement in daily life?

Sankara resolves this controversy in an ingenious manner. While he puts Gyanamarg and monasticism on the pedestal, he also affirms explicitly on several occasions that it is only through the continuous practice of Karmamarg that man can acquire the qualities necessary to traverse on Gyanamarg. He looked upon Karmamarg as the purifier of man and as paving the way for Gyanamarg. (See Chapter VIII).   At the same time Sankara also held open the possibility of Gyanamarg being embraced at an early stage itself in one's life, provided the person concerned possessed the Knowledge to discriminate between the transcendent and temporal, between finite and infinite. But this was clearly beyond the ken of ordinary man. Sankara in this way prescribed Karmamarg for the overwhelming majority who were unable to differentiate the body from the Soul. To sum up, Sankara espoused both Gyanamarg and Karmamarg; while extolling monasticism he saw much merit in worldly existence. Sankara thus blends in a harmonious way the teachings of Sramanism, Buddhism, Jainism, and Samkhyaism as well as of Hindu texts pertaining to the prescription of the ideal way of life for man.

1:	*Indian Philosophy. By Dr. S. Radhakrishnan. Volume 1, Oxford University Press. Page 352*
2:	*Brahma-Sutra Bhashya. Translation by Swami Gambhirananda. Advaita Ashrama. 5, Delhi, Entally Road. Calcutta. 700014. Pages 333 & 334*

3:       Ibid. Page 334
4:       A history of early Vedanta Philosophy by Hajime Nekamura.
         Published by Motilal Banarsidass. Pages 285 &286. Quotation
         slightly amended by the author for clarity.
5:       FN. 1. Ibid. Vol. II. Page 284
6:       FN. 2. Ibid. Page 858
7:       FN. I. Ibid. Page 286
8:       FN. 2. Ibid. pages 154 & 155